The police and the public in England and Wales: A British Crime Survey Report

by Wesley G. Skogan

A HOME OFFICE
RESEARCH AND PLANNING UNIT
REPORT

LONDON : HMSO

ISBN 0 11 340995 8

HOME OFFICE RESEARCH STUDIES

"Home Office Research Studies" comprise reports on research undertaken in the Home Office to assist in the exercise of its administrative functions, and for the information of the judicature, the services for which the Home Secretary has responsibility (direct or indirect) and the general public.

On the last pages of this report are listed titles already published in this series, in the preceding series Studies in the Causes of Delinquency and the Treatment of Offenders, and in the series of Research and Planning Unit Papers.

Her Majesty's Stationery Office

Standing order service

Placing a standing order with HMSO BOOKS enables a customer to receive other titles in this series automatically as published.

This saves time, trouble and expense of placing individual orders and avoids the problem of knowing when to do so.

For details please write to HMSO BOOKS (PC13A/1), Publications Centre, P.O. Box 276, London SW8 5DT and quoting reference 25.08.011.

The standing order service also enables customers to receive automatically as published all material of their choice which additionally saves extensive catalogue research. The scope and selectivity of the service has been extended by new techniques, and there are more than 3,500 classifications to choose from. A special leaflet describing the service in detail may be obtained on request.

Foreword

This report is the second in the Home Office Research Studies series to present findings from the 1988 British Crime Survey (BCS). The first report offered information about the nature and extent of selected crimes, and the different groups at risk. This study examines the whole range of people's contacts with the police, whether or not connected with crime. This is the second sweep of the BCS to look in detail at the public's attitude towards the police. A police component was also included in the 1982 survey.

The BCS shows that the public has a great deal of confidence in the police (85 per cent rated their performance as 'good' or 'very good'). At the same time there has been a steady erosion of confidence over the past decade. The survey suggests that there is a gap — which is perhaps widening — between the public's expectations about the capacity of the police and their actual ability to deliver services. The report points out, however, that the public's expectations of the police may be unrealistically high.

The survey found that people's experiences of the police and assessment of the services they provided were consistently related to factors such as age, race and gender. Members of the ethnic minorities were particularly dissatisfied with the way their cases were handled when they contacted the police, and with how politely they were treated when stopped in the street. The report also looks at the responsibility of the public to help the police combat crime by reporting their own experiences to the police, and stepping forward as witnesses when they see crime occurring. The BCS indicates that the public are frequently reluctant to contact the police in either capacity and concludes that more attention needs to be paid to identifying the reasons for this reluctance and overcoming it.

ROGER TARLING
Head of the Research and Planning Unit

Acknowledgements

The British Crime Survey represents the effort of a number of people. It was conceived of and directed by the staff of the Research and Planning Unit of the Home Office. Mike Hough developed the policing component of the questionnaire, and Julie Vennard provided direction in the analysis of the data on police contacts. Pat Mayhew and David Elliott provided the data that was specially analysed for this report. All of this proceeded with the support of Mary Tuck, then Head of the Research and Planning Unit. The sampling and data collection were conducted by NOP Market Research and Social and Community Planning Research. Douglas Wood of SCPR played an important role in the development of the BCS as well as in the 1988 survey; all of those involved with the BCS mourn his death. Thanks are also due to Michael G. Maxfield, who provided detailed comments (not all of which were taken to heart) on a preliminary draft of this report.

WESLEY G. SKOGAN

Contents

1 Introduction

This report examines the extent of public contact with police, and some of the consequences of their encounters. It is based upon the findings of the third sweep of the British Crime Survey (BCS), which was conducted in February and March of 1988. Police are the most visible agency of local government. The BCS indicates that in a little over a year almost 60 per cent of the adult population has some occasion to come into contact with them. They live in the community, and many people are personally acquainted with police officers. Unlike many sectors of government, issues involving the police and crime also ignite the imagination of the public. People are interested in what police do (or in what they think they do), and the quality of police service can make a difference in their lives. Unlike some other agencies, police depend upon the active co-operation of the public to get their job done. They need to be notified promptly of crimes and other emergencies, and members of the public must be willing to step forward when they have information which would be useful in their investigations. Therefore, what the public think of the police is of more than casual interest. They care about the quality of policing. Most have at least some basis for making a judgment about police performance, and the police need their confidence.

By and large, public confidence in the police is high. The BCS asked all respondents if they thought the police in their area did a very good job, a fairly good job, a fairly poor job, or very poor job; 85 per cent rated them as fairly or very good. When asked to compare police in their area to other places in the country, more thought they were better than average than thought they were worse.

However, while the public has a great deal of confidence in the police, there is also some reason for concern about the direction in which opinion is moving. Three sweeps of the BCS have revealed something of an erosion in support for police. The first, in 1982, found that 92 per cent of the residents of England and Wales who had an opinion about the police rated their performance as good or very good; in 1984 the comparable figure was 90 per cent, and in 1988 it was 85 per cent. More ominously, the percentage giving them the highest marks has dropped from 43 per cent in 1982 to only 25 per cent in 1988[1]. Comparisons of

---

[1] These figures differ from those in Mayhew, Elliott and Dowds, 1989, where levels of satisfaction with police performance are expressed including respondents who said they did not have an opinion. On this basis, in 1982 75 per cent said they thought police performance was 'very or fairly good', 83 per cent in 1984, and 75 per cent in 1988. The figures for those who said police performance was 'very good' were 35 per cent in 1982, 31 per cent in 1984 and 22 per cent in 1988. The proportion of people who did not have an opinion was 19 per cent in 1982, seven per cent in 1984 and 13 per cent in 1988.

the three BCS surveys indicate that confidence has fallen in almost every type of community and in many important social categories. The percentage of persons who think police do a 'very good job' has declined the most in small towns and rural areas, among women and the elderly, and among whites — all groups which traditionally have been the most supportive of the police. (A detailed tabulation of changing attitudes toward the police is presented in Table B-1 in Appendix B.)

This decline in general satisfaction with policing is consistent with the findings of independent opinion polls. For example, surveys by Market & Opinion Research International have found that the proportion of the public that is satisfied with policing in their area has declined by 17 percentage points (from 75 per cent to 58 per cent) between 1981 and 1989. The largest drop was between polls conducted in 1985 and 1987. The proportion of the population choosing the police as one of the two or three occupations they have the most respect for has fallen from 54 per cent to 42 per cent during the same period (British Public Opinion, 1989). Their ranking is still high compared to many other occupations and groups (it is higher, for example, than respect for teachers, scientists, and MPs), and some of this decline doubtless reflects general perceptions of public institutions. However, it comes in the face of a long tradition that the police are among the most trusted occupational groups (Hough, 1989).

A substantial proportion of the public also is uninformed about police activities. When asked to rate the general quality of police performance, 13 per cent (who were not counted in the figures above) would not venture an opinion about whether it was good or poor, and 28 per cent could not compare police in their area to others elsewhere. Twenty per cent could not hazard a guess as to whether the number of police patrols in their area had gone up or down over time.

This report examines the public's opinion of the police in the light of their experience with them. There are many sources of opinion which are out of the hands of government, but people's actual encounters with police play an important role in shaping what they think of the institution. How people are treated in individual cases makes a difference. The BCS provides a vehicle for assessing the nature of public contacts with police among a large and representative sample of the population. The survey allows them to describe why and how they encountered the police, what happened, and their assessment of how the matter was handled. The results shed some light on the factors which underlie public support for the police, and suggest some ideas for improving the state of police/public relations.

Structure of the report

Chapter 2 looks first at the extent to which the public relies on the police for protection and assistance. It examines the distribution of their telephone and personal contacts with police, including both emergency and non-emergency matters. It explores the sources of public satisfaction and dissatisfaction with those encounters. Appendix A details some of the analytic and statistical decisions lying behind this and later chapters. Chapter 3 turns to police initiated contacts with the public. Although they involve many fewer people, these have more potential for conflict. Most involve traffic stops and vehicle checks, but the survey also included respondents who had been stopped and questioned by police while they were on the street. This chapter examines what came of these encounters, and people's perceptions of how they were treated. Chapter 4 investigates two important roles for the public in combating crime: reporting their own experiences of crime to the police, and stepping forward as witnesses when they see crime occurring. The BCS indicates that the public could do a great deal more in both regards. Chapter 5 reviews the findings of the report, and Appendix B presents some of the detailed statistical tabulations on which they are based.

About the BCS

The 1988 BCS questioned residents of about 10,500 randomly selected households in England and Wales.[2] They were chosen to be a representative cross-section of persons aged 16 or over living in private households whose addresses appear in the electoral register. People living in institutions were not sampled. In addition to being asked a common core of questions about their experiences of crime, about one half of those interviewed then were asked about efforts they had taken to protect themselves and their families against victimisation. The remainder were questioned about their contacts with police. The questions about the police largely focused on experiences they had during 1987 and the two or three months in 1988 which preceded the interviewer's visit to their home.

Those who were questioned about police had a great deal to report, for 59 per cent had had some recent contact with them. During the interview, respondents were asked whether they had telephoned the police, visited a police station, or approached an officer on the street, and if police had stopped them while they were on the street or in the car. If they recalled any of these kinds of contacts, they were then questioned about why they contacted the police or why they were stopped, what the police did and how they were treated, and how satisfied or dissatisfied they were with manner in which the police handled the matter. The interview also included several general questions about their knowledge of police, their assessments of police performance at a number of tasks, and official complaints which the respondents might have tried to make concerning police behaviour. This report focuses mainly on the relationship between people's experiences of the police and their assessments of how they were treated. Many of the more general questions included in the policing supplement to the 1988 BCS are not examined here. However, this focus on concrete situations is likely

---

[2]A detailed description of the survey samples and procedures can be found in Mayhew, Elliott and Dowds, 1989; 86-96.

to elicit people's most firmly held beliefs about the police and reflect their clearest perceptions of police behaviour, and as such should provide the firmest ground for assessing police performance (see Hough, 1989).

The randomly selected sample of almost 5,000 residents of England and Wales who were questioned about the police was sufficiently large to examine most of the questions of interest here. The interviews turned up only a small number of persons (137) who had been stopped and questioned while they were on foot, but otherwise various kinds of contacts with the police were well represented. However, there has been a great deal of interest in the dealings of significant ethnic minorities — notably, Afro-Caribbeans and Asians — with the police. Because of their small numbers in the population they will not be well enough represented in a general survey to shed much light on their experiences. To remedy this, the 1988 BCS also included a special, add-on sample of ethnic minorities. They answered the core questionnaire, and the supplementary questions concerning the police. In all, 841 Asians and 641 Afro-Caribbeans were questioned, as well as 4,700 whites. The majority of Asians were of Indian origin (59 per cent) or from Pakistan (32 per cent); the remainder were Bangladeshi. These proportions closely match those revealed by the National Labour Force Survey and other estimates of the composition of the population. The regular BCS sample also included Chinese and other Oriental respondents, but they were too few in number (38 in all) to examine separately. Discussions in this report which focus on ethnicity are based on the combined regular and supplemental samples, while all other analyses draw only upon the representative sample. All of the tables are based on data which were weighted slightly to make them more representative of the population. The survey deliberately oversampled inner city residents, who were therefore downweighted slightly, and small weights also adjusted the sample for mismatches between the electoral register and the actual number of adults who turned out to be living at the selected addresses.

2 Serving the public

The police provide a broad range of services, reflecting the diverse nature of the demands placed upon them by the public. A large proportion of their workload is determined by the volume and nature of requests for police service made directly by the public, either by telephone or by approaching them personally. Some of these cases involve terrifying or life-threatening emergencies, but most do not. More of them involve crimes of some sort, but a surprising number do not fall directly in that category either. This chapter examines who contacts the police, how and why they do so, and how the police respond. The police must deal with these situations, but do not always do so to the satisfaction of those who contacted them. People in different areas rely on the police for help with different kinds of problems, and this is reflected in how they are served and their assessments of the quality of police performance.

Who relies on the police?

One goal of the BCS was to document the extent to which the public relies on the police. To do so, the survey questioned people about several different kinds of encounters they might have had with them. These questions focused only on events which had occurred during the 14 months or so between January, 1987 and the day of the interview, so that people's recollections of events would be sharper. They were questioned about telephoning the 999 police emergency number (nine per cent had done so), telephoning a police station directly (26 per cent), visiting a station personally (23 per cent), approaching an officer on the street or in another public place (23 per cent), and 'other' public initiated contacts (five per cent). Excluding overlaps between these kinds of experiences, 56 per cent of those interviewed had initiated at least one contact with the police during the previous 14 months.

The distribution of these contacts is summarised in Table 1, which describes the backgrounds of this who contacted the police in any way[1]. This summary is useful because these contacts were patterned in fairly similar ways across police station telephone calls and visits, and personal conversations.

The general message of Table 1 is that public initiated contacts with the police were more common among better off people. The frequency of contacts with the police declines steadily the further down the income, occupational, and educational ladder one looks. Measures of several other social and economic factors which are not included in Table 1, such as social class, pointed in the same

---

[1] For a discussion of statistical issues, see Appendix A.

direction. On the other hand, there were virtually no differences in the frequency with which Afro-Caribbeans and whites approached the police, but Asians were less likely to be in contact. Asians in particular, were less likely to approach the police personally — in public or by visiting a police station — or than their counterparts. As Table 1 indicates, there were no substantial differences between rural and urban areas in the frequency of these police/public contacts. Contacts of all kinds were distinctively less common among those over 60, but otherwise there were no great age differences in public initiated police contacts. The pattern described in Table 1 is very similar to the findings of other studies, including the Policy Studies Institute's survey of London in 1981 (Smith, 1983). Table B-2 in Appendix B presents a detailed demographic breakdown of the verious forms of police/public contacts. There was a tendency for Afro-Caribbeans, Asians, and inner city residents to use the 999 emergency number more often than others. Otherwise, the distribution of 999 calls generally did not vary much from group to group (the number of cases in each was often small). The remaining forms of contact with police were distributed fairly uniformly over the groups listed in Table 1. Most of the factors presented in Table 1 are related to one another as well as to contacts with police. For example, ethnic minorities — especially Afro-Caribbeans — are heavily concentrated in inner city areas; in addition, residents in those areas tend to have distinctive experiences and attitudes regardless of race[2]. Appendix A describes how multivariate statistics were used to disentangle the correlation between those and other factors. Such a multivariate analysis of contacts with the police (presented in Table B-3) shows the relative importance of the various factors in Table 1 in statistically describing which BCS respondents contacted the police during 1987. The most important factors were ethnicity and gender (Asians and women had fewer contacts), followed by age, status, and housing arrangements. Afro-Carribeans and whites continued to resemble one another, and there were no significant differences between cities and rural areas in rates of contact. Another factor which was strongly related to contacting police was victimisation. Slightly over 70 per cent of the crime victims interviewed in 1988 had been in contact with the police (although not necessarily about every incident), as contrasted to 47 per cent of those who had not been victimised. Although victimisation was also related to most of the factors presented in Table 1, this link was independent of the other factors, as indicated in Table B-3.

The findings summarised in Table 1 belie two widespread myths about police. It frequently is assumed that the police principally serve the poor and disadvantaged, because of the concentration of crime-related problems in their neighbourhoods and because other means of solving their problems do not come easily to hand. It is also often argued (for example, Shapland and Vagg, 1987) that city residents rely most heavily upon the police, while in less populated areas

[2]A detailed profile of the social and economic backgrounds of white, Afro-Caribbean, and Asian respondents in the BCS can be found in Mayhew, Elliott, and Dowds, 1989.

there are fewer crime problems and a greater spirit of neighbourly concern and assistance for people to draw upon when they do need aid. Neither of those observations fits the findings of the BCS. Instead, it is people who are closer to the top of the social ladder than the bottom that contact the police most often, and they are as quick to do so in rural areas and small towns as in the inner cities. It seems that popular stereotypes about what people rely on the police *for* are often wrong.

Table 1

Groups contacting police

Group	Per cent contacting	(N)	Group	Per cent contacting	(N)
RACE			OCCUPATION STATUS **		
whites	56	(4636)	semi/unskilled	46	(986)
Afro-Caribbeans	57	(510)	skilled manual	54	(1381)
Asians	47**	(736)	non-managerial	62	(854)
			professional	64	(1388)
AGE **					
16-24	60	(722)	HOUSING **		
25-29	66	(408)	council housing	47	(1061)
30-44	65	(1290)	all others	58	(3737)
45-59	60	(1148)			
60 plus	38	(1266)	AREA OF RESIDENCE		
			inner city	55	(846)
INCOME **			metropolitan	54	(1041)
under £10,000	48	(1800)	urbanised area	57	(922)
£10-£19,999	67	(1175)	mixed areas	56	(1091)
£20,000 or more	74	(611)	rural areas	58	(958)
GENDER **			LEFT SCHOOL **		
males	63	(2340)	under age 15	38	(1167)
females	49	(2518)	all others	62	(3642)
ALL RESPONDENTS					
	56	(4858)			

Weighted data. ** indicates significant multivariate relationship controlling for other factors in the table. (For a discussion of tests of significance, see Appendix A.) For an analysis by type of contact, see Table B-2.**

Why they call upon police

The popular image is that people turn to the police principally regarding crime problems, and that the bulk of those situations are emergencies. Instead, the BCS shows that most police/public contacts are not about crises, but that they involve many other kinds of problems, and that many of them do not involve 'problems' at all. These findings explain part of the social distribution of police contacts described in Table 1.

7

A sketch of the reasons that BCS respondents gave for contacting the police is presented in Table 2. When people telephoned (or, less frequently, visited) a police station concerning crimes which had struck them, their families, or other people, they are classified in Table 2 as having 'reported a crime'. The crime category in Table 2 includes vandalism and domestic violence, as well as property thefts and other forms of personal crime. Another category includes complaints concerning suspicious people or circumstances, nuisances, loud parties and other disturbances, or ringing burglar alarms (hereafter these will all be referred to as 'disturbances'). Upon investigation some of these might have involved criminal offences, but they could not be clearly labelled as such by those initially reporting them. Many people also contacted the police to give them information concerning stray animals, traffic accidents or road obstructions, gas leaks, floods, fires, and other non-crime emergencies; these make up another category in Table 2. Reports of crimes or disturbances, and efforts to give information to the police, most frequently were made by telephone. In contrast, a large number of people are classified in Table 2 as visiting police stations or approaching individual officers to *ask* questions (for directions, or the time) or to *get* advice. Some also visited the police station because they had to deliver documents to the police; these included registration forms and insurance certificates for their vehicles, and their driving licences if they had been unable to show them when asked to do so by a police officer. In addition, a large number of respondents recalled having a social chat with an officer on the street.

Table 2 classifies each of these *reasons* for making a contact and, *how* it was done. For example, a little less than a third of telephone calls to the police 999 emergency number involved specific criminal incidents, while about equal numbers involved disturbances or efforts to give information to the police. On the other hand, almost half of the public encounters between citizens and police involved social chats.

Table 2 indicates that the bulk of public initiated contacts with police did not directly concern crime. The summary column shows only about 18 per cent involved specific crime incidents. An additional 12 per cent of all contacts concerned disturbances of one kind or another, but even adding those failed to raise the count to one third of the total. The definition of what is 'crime related contact' and how it is made varies somewhat from study to study, but this figure is consistent with a series of studies of citizen contacts with police, which are nicely summarised by Jones *et al.* (1986) and Clarke and Hough (1984). The total of crime and disturbance calls was higher for 999 contacts than for others (making up about two thirds of them), but other research suggests that many or most of those also did not involve real emergencies. For example, Smith (1983) found that only for ten per cent of 999 calls did Londoners recall that they truly felt worried or at risk. The routine nature of many contacts is also reflected in studies of telephone calls from the point of view of the police radio controllers who receive them. Most involve administrative matters, requests for information, nuisances, troubles with children, lost or found property, disputes, or incidents in the past; only a very small percentage (two – five per cent in some studies) turn out to be serious and require an immediate police response (Ekblom and Heal, 1982).

According to the BCS, more contacts with the police involved exchanging information, apparently of a non-crime and largely non-emergency nature. In about 16 per cent of these cases people were reporting traffic accidents or obstructions to police, reporting a missing animal, or letting police know that their home would be empty. Another 23 per cent involved requesting information *from* police, about lost or found property, directions, and even the time of day. Information sharing of this sort constituted almost 40 per cent of these police/public contacts.

Table 2

Why the public contacted police

Per cent reporting each reason	*Telephoned 999*	*station*	*Visited station*	*Spoke to in public*	*Total*
report a crime	31	32	13	2	18
give police information	30	20	15	8	16
ask police for information	—	3	46	33	23
social chat	—	—	—	49	14
disturbance, suspicion, alarm	33	21	2	2	12
required to do so by police	—	—	23	—	7
other	6	24	1	5	10
TOTAL PER CENT	100	100	100	99	100
(N)	(440)	(1229)	(1142)	(1118)	(3929)

Weighted data. One column does not sum to 100 per cent due to rounding.

These national figures are not in close agreement with the findings of inner city victimisation surveys of the London Borough of Islington (Jones, *et al*, 1986) and of Merseyside (Kinsey, 1985). They report much higher ratios of crime to non-crime contacts with police. The Islington crime survey found that 51 per cent of contacts with police concerned crime, and 56 per cent either crime or disturbances (Jones *et al.*, 1986: Table 3.15); the figures for Merseyside were even higher. This crime/non-crime ratio of virtually 1:1 differs dramatically from the national 1:5 figure revealed here. It is also greater than the 1:3 ratio which characterises many studies of contacts with the police.

The high proportion of crime-related contacts found in the Islington and Merseyside studies was put forward to challenge an emerging consensus among police researchers that the bulk of police work involves non-crime, non-emergency problems. Jones *et al.*, (1986) juxtapose their high ratios to other research in Britain and the United States in order to argue that an emphasis on service-oriented policing does not respond to the priorities of the residents of the poor inner city areas they studied. They argue that police should prioritise crime control and be held responsible for how well they do it, and imply that discussions of non-crime, non-emergency policing are a cover-up for declining police effectiveness at solving crimes.

One reason for the discrepancy between BCS and local survey figures on the amount of crime contact could simply be questionnaire difference (ie. tight comparisons are only possible when the range of 'contact alternatives' is exactly the same). More important, an obvious difference is that the figures presented here are national whereas those from Islington and Merseyside relate to inner city areas. Indeed, when the reasons for which people contact police are broken down by size of place, a larger proportion of inner city contacts involve crime and disturbances. This can be seen in Table 3. Like almost all of the tabulations in this report it is based on persons, and presents, for each subgroup of the population, the number of people who contacted the police concerning crime as a percentage of all those who contacted the police. It excludes the 'social chats' described in Table 2, and counts (as it did above) vandalism and domestic disputes as crimes (in some studies they are included in the disturbance category). Table 3 also includes information on contacts concerning disturbances, and gives the combined total as well. As Reiner (1985) notes, people may need help to deal with disturbances which have slipped beyond their control, and this can be the province of the police.

A number of social and economic factors were related to the reasons people gave for contacting police (see Table 3). Asians were significantly more likely to contact them concerning crime problems (for a similar finding, see Smith, 1983), as were residents of council housing and higher risk areas[3]. BCS interviewers' ratings of the quality of housing in each respondent's immediate vicinity were only weakly related to contacts with police. Contacts concerning crime problems were dominated by area of residence, and they dropped off sharply in villages and rural areas. The effect of other factors disappeared on controlling for location. Reports of disturbances also were concentrated in inner cities and other urban

---

[3]BCS respondents were grouped by the ACORN classification for the area they lived in; these in turn were characterised by the victimisation rate for that ACORN class. For a description of ACORN classifications, see Hough and Mayhew, 1985; for a discussion of their grouping by victimisation rates, see Mayhew, Elliott and Dowds, 1989.

areas, but in addition whites and older people were significantly more likely than others to contact the police concerning disturbances.

Table 3

Percentage of contacts concerning crime and disturbances

		Per cent reporting:—		*Number of*
Group	crime	disturbances	both	police contacts
RACE				
whites	27	19	44	(2253)
Afro-Caribbeans	31	9 **	40	(252)
Asians	39 *	13 **	50 *	(316)
AGE CATEGORY		**	*	
16-24	26	10	36	(383)
25-29	28	16	43	(239)
30-44	28	20	46	(735)
45-59	29	19	46	(605)
60 plus	22	23	44	(376)
HOUSING	*		*	
council housing	31	19	49	(425)
all others	26	18	43	(1919)
AREA HOUSING				
mostly good	26	18	43	(1537)
mostly fair	28	18	46	(666)
bad/very bad	32	17	48	(73)
AREA CRIME RISK	*		*	
high risk	31	18	49	(906)
low risk	24	19	41	(1435)
AREA OF RESIDENCE	**	**	**	
inner city	37	21	54	(403)
metropolitan	29	18	46	(504)
urbanised	28	21	48	(444)
mixed areas	22	16	38	(535)
rural areas	21	16	36	(458)
ALL RESPONDENTS	27	18	44	(2341)

Weighted data.   ** indicates significant multivariate relationship controlling for other factors in the table;   * indicates a significant bivariate relationship.

In summary, a large proportion of the public's contacts with police are not about specific crime problems, and the vast majority do not involve emergencies. This varied mostly by location, and there clearly is a need to examine the mix of demands on local police services. Residents in higher risk, inner city areas, for instance, face most crime problems. Nationally, only about three per cent of the contacts summarised in Table 2 (those in the upper left-hand corner) were 999 calls concerning particular crime incidents.

11

Instead, most public initiated encounters reflected the integration of the police into the routines of everyday life. They were called upon to preserve tranquility, ease the flow of traffic, serve as a clearing house for reports of a variety of community problems, assist in civil emergencies, and help people find their way. Quantitatively, these forms of police service are by far the most frequently requested, and they are the principal kind of contact that most of the population has with their police. How well they are served in these ways may have a very large impact on the public as a consequence.

Frequency of contacts

Most of those who contacted the police during 1987 and early 1988 did so only once or twice. Whatever their concerns, they were not driven repeatedly to summon police or approach them personally for support, assistance, or advice. However, of the 56 per cent of the population who did contact police, 28 per cent (or 16 per cent of the population) did so three times or more during that period. They were 'heavy consumers' of policing, and the BCS can tell us something about who they were.

Using as the definition of a 'heavy consumer' anyone contacting the police three times or more in a year, 11 per cent of those using 999 and 23 per cent of those who telephoned police stations directly were heavy consumers of service. About 14 per cent of those who made station visits and 36 per cent of persons who approached officers in public did so three times or more as well. An analysis of the correlates of multiple contacts is presented in Table B-3. Asians reported fewer repeat contacts, males and higher-status people reported somewhat more, and they were a bit more frequent in small towns and rural areas. Of all the users of police services, crime victims were more likely than non-victims to make repeat contacts. This was true across all major categories of crime, and especially among victims of assault. In addition to the figures presented in the tables, there also was a tendency for both owners and managers of small businesses (those with 1 to 24 employees) to contact the police repeatedly; 41 per cent had done so. They also had a higher likelihood of making one or more contacts (79 per cent had such encounters during the previous 14 months). It is possible that this high rate of contact with police reflects their supervisory responsibilities and their exposure to the general public.

The police response

The BCS can shed only a little light on just what the police did in response to the public's complaints and the information they brought them. The BCS provides a 'consumer' perspective on police operations — interviewers asked those who were involved to describe encounters with the police, from their point of view. The BCS was not designed to gather extensive details about police practices (for example, how fast they came when summoned, or what they did at the scene). These are known, however, to affect people's perceptions of the quality of the service they have received (Ekblom & Heal, 1982). The BCS *did* ask how satisfied they were with the way the police handled their matter, and, if they were dissatisfied, the reasons why[4].

There are naturally some limitations to using such perceptual measures of performance. Some respondents doubtless misjudged what the police were doing, and others may have let their past opinions about the police affect their views. Some undoubtedly had forgotten exactly what happened by the time a BCS interviewer came to their door. Just as importantly, the officers handling their case may have had very good reasons for doing what they did, even if those reasons were poorly communicated (or not communicated at all) to the parties involved. For example, their district might have been short-staffed, requiring them to deal seemingly too quickly with many matters. It is the nature of 'market research' that it only uncovers what consumers think about the service they have received, but unlike general questions about the police, those examined here concerned specific and recent events about which respondents could have had an opinion which was rooted in their experience. These are more likely to provide a valid basis for evaluating police performance.

Like the rest of the public, those who contacted the police during 1987 mostly were pleased with their performance. However, when they were questioned in detail about specific recent encounters with the police, as many as 20 per cent indicated they were dissatisfied with what had transpired. The most satisfied were those who had approached an officer in public (only eight per cent were dissatisfied with these contacts); the most dissatisfied were those who used the 999 emergency number (18 per cent) or telephoned a local police station (20 per cent). Discovering some of the immediate causes of this dissatisfaction is the goal of the remainder of this chapter.

Patterns of satisfaction

Table 4 describes several factors associated with people's satisfaction concerning their experiences of the police. Some (race, age, place of residence) have to do with who they are and where they live. Others are concerned with why they contacted the police and what was done in response. All of these turned out to be important in understanding people's assessments of what occurred when they telephoned or approached the police.

First, Table 4 documents a large gulf between whites and racial minorities, and between younger and older people, in their degree of satisfaction with police contacts. Residents of larger cities were also consistently less satisfied with police performance. As Table 4 indicates, these differences persisted when they all were taken into account at the same time. For example, inner city residents of all races

---

[4]Respondents who just had 'social chats' with police (see Table 2) were not asked follow up questions, and are excluded from discussions of satisfaction with specific police/public encounters. While there was no evidence about the effects of this, it seems likely that people who initiated these conversations would more frequently be satisfied than dissatisfied with them. Although their importance in shaping public attitudes is uncertain, the exclusion of social contacts may bias the findings reported in the final column of Table 4.

were less satisfied than the population as a whole with police responses, and in addition there were substantial differences between the races. Variations in satisfaction with the police can also be found among factors not shown in Table 4; for example, men, the unemployed, and less educated people were also less positive than others. The significance of these demographic factors persists when other features of these encounters are controlled for; this is documented in Table B-5 in Appendix B.

Table 4 also shows large differences in levels of satisfaction related to *why* people summon or approach the police. In every instance, those who were concerned about crime problems were the least satisfied. They were followed by those who contacted the police to report disturbances, a group that Ekblom and Heal (1982) also found to be less satisfied with the response of the police. As Jones *et al.,* (1986: 116) concluded, this implies in a general way that 'the less urgent the matter the more satisfied the public'. Getting and giving information, on the other hand, clearly generated much more positive responses. These differences were very strong in multivariate analyses controlling for many other factors (separate measures were used for each reason, contrasting their effect against the 'other' and 'get information' categories). It also turns out that the most common criticisms of the quality of police service — including how much effort they put into solving the problem and their success at doing so — are most relevant to contacts concerning crime and disturbances. The next section of this chapter examines the relationship between 'reasons for contact' and level of satisfaction more closely.

Table 4 indicates whether or not the complainant actually had face to face contact with the police was related to levels of satisfaction. According to those interviewed in the BCS, they met an officer face to face 56 per cent of the time when they contacted the police via a 999 call, and 50 per cent of the time when they telephoned a local police station[5]. It may seem surprising that only just over half of those people who make 999 calls actually encounter an officer, but many studies of the use of police emergency lines confirm that they are frequently used to make enquiries, to report non-crime matters, to report long-past events, and to check on incidents which had already been reported. As a result, Ekblom and Heal (1982) found that police radio controllers found it necessary to fill out a fresh crime incident report for only 18 per cent of calls, and often did not have to dispatch a patrol officer. When BCS respondents telephoned concerning crime (which does not necessarily imply a crisis), the police met them personally almost 80 per cent of the time; the comparable figure for disturbances was 46 per cent, and when they called to give the police information of some sort it was 36 per cent. The majority of the crime-related cases in which they did not meet callers involved vandalism.

---

[5]These figures differ somewhat from those presented in Mayhew, Elliott, and Dowds, 1989. Theirs are based on crime incidents, while these are based on each respondent's most recent contacts by telephone, regardless of the subject.

Further, there were doubtless many occasions in which police dealt with the problems that were reported to them without having to meet the complainant. However, people were more satisfied when the police met them, regardless of the reason they telephoned. This difference proved to be significant even when other important sources of satisfaction were controlled for; it appears to be as important as race differences, and about twice as important as the effect of gender, as will be documented in a section below.

Table 4
Satisfaction with public initiated encounters

Group	Telephoned 999	Visited station	Visited station	Spoke to in public
RACE†				
whites	53	47	53	69
Afro-Caribbeans	28**	33**	31**	62
Asians	21**	26**	28**	52*
AGE	**	**	**	
16-24	39	30	38	76
25-29	30	34	44	81
30-44	48	47	54	63
45 plus	60	54	62	66
PLACE OF RESIDENCE	**	**	**	*
inner city	44	37	45	64
metro areas	50	42	51	65
urban areas	51	44	47	71
mixed areas	60	52	56	68
rural areas	64	55	63	74
REASON FOR CONTACT				
about crime	39**	28**	24**	45**
disturbances	49**	43**	52**	50**
give information	66**	56**	61	50**
get information	—	73	62	75
POLICE RESPONSE	**	**		
no face to face contact	47	46	—	—
face to face	56	50	—	—
ALL RESPONDENTS	52	47	52	68
(N)	(414)	(1189)	(1130)	(564)

Weighted data. ** indicates significant multivariate relationship controlling for other factors in the table; * indicates a significant bivariate relationship. For the multivariate analysis, see Table B-5. † Race includes minority booster sample.

All of the factors described in Table 4 were related to *each other* as well as to satisfaction, sometimes in complex ways. For example, Afro-Caribbeans were more likely to telephone the police concerning crime, while whites more frequently contacted them concerning disturbances. The police were more likely to meet complainants when telephoned about crime than about disturbances, however, and these contradictory effects to a certain extent cancel one another out. Table 4 flags those relationships which were independent of the effects of other factors described in the Table, and the conclusion of this chapter attempts to tie all of them together.

Table 4 does not present a complete account of the correlates of satisfaction with public initiated police contacts. The heavy consumers of policing were somewhat less satisfied with their experiences than those who contacted them only once or twice during 1987. Those who telephoned 999 with high frequency were particularly likely to be less satisfied with how their latest encounter was handled by the police. Also, Maxfield (1988) found that respondents in the 1982 BCS who had been stopped on foot, arrested, or charged with some offence were more dissatisfied when they later contacted police in the role of victim. Ekblom and Heal (1982) found a similar pattern among people who telephoned the police. Some categories of crime involve large numbers of victims who have themselves been in trouble with the police. For example, the 1982 BCS included a section on self-reported offending, and found that assault victims were seven times more likely than others to have been offenders as well (Gottfredson, 1984). These victims may be more hesitant about contacting police, more circumspect in their dealings with them, and more critical in their views. Finally, there was little evidence in the 1988 BCS of what the police *did* when they were contacted. There is no description of what they did if they came to the scene of an incident, or if they reacted in some affirmative way to information which was brought to their personal attention. Research to be summarised below indicates that these are also important determinants of public satisfaction with police service.

Sources of dissatisfaction

If anyone who had been in contact with police indicated some dissatisfaction with their performance, they were asked for details about the case. Table 5 summarises the nature of those complaints about police performance, while a detailed breakdown of complaints by type of contact is presented in Table B-4 in Appendix B. The first category involved allegations of an apparent lack of effort on their part. About one third of those with a specific complaint mentioned a seeming lack of interest by the police in their case, and 42 per cent judged that the police did not do enough. Those complaints overlapped (respondents could make more than one), but fully 53 per cent of all those who complained mentioned a problem in this category.

Dissatisfaction caused by an apparent lack of effort by police was so common that it predominated in every demographic category, and it was the most common source of dissatisfaction for every type of contact. There was a tendency

16

for overlapping categories of Afro-Caribbeans Asians, those in the lower status occupational categories, the unemployed, and urban dwellers to register this objection more often. However, this was by far the most commonly expressed source of dissatisfaction in *every* age group, among all races and occupational categories, by men and women, and in large cities and in rural areas. It was especially prominent among those who contacted the police by telephone, using either 999 or a regular police number. However, it is important to note that in terms of absolute numbers the largest problem is not a widespread one. This can be seen in the second and third columns of Table 5, which indicate how frequently each major category of remarks was made by: (a) all of those who contacted the police and (b) the population as a whole. By these measures, there were relatively few objections concerning police performance and demeanour, even in the most common categories. The largest source of dissatisfaction — an apparent lack of effort — was reported by only nine per cent of those who contacted the police, and by five per cent of the general population.

Table 5

Dissatisfaction with police performance

	Per cent of complainants who mentioned each complaint	Complainant as per cent of contacts	Complainant as per cent of population
1. APPARENT LACK OF EFFORT	53	9	5
(i) were not interested	34		
(ii) did not do enough	42		
2. POOR PERFORMANCE	30	5	3
(i) could not answer query	7		
(ii) made mistakes	11		
(iii) did not apprehend anyone	15		
(iv) did not recover property	8		
3. MADE RESPONDENT WAIT	14	2	1
4. DID NOT KEEP INFORMED	18	3	2
5. BEHAVED IMPOLITELY	11	2	1
6. OTHER	25	4	2
ANY SPECIFIC COMPLAINT	100	17	10

Weighted data. Based on 417 main sample respondents, who registered a total of 866 complaints. For a breakdown of complaints by type of contact, see Table B-4. Percentage of complainants who mentioned each complaint does not add up to 100 per cent due to multiple responses.

The next large category of remarks focused on how well the police did their job. Together, these complaints were made by about 30 per cent of those who were dissatisfied. Some who had contacted the police were dissatisfied because they had questions that were not answered, while others judged that the police made mistakes in handling their case. Victims also were unhappy because the police did not apprehend anyone, or because their property was not recovered.

The remaining categories of complaints, that the police made respondents wait, that they did not keep them adequately informed about the progress of their case, and that they behaved impolitely, were less frequently made. The belief that they had to wait too long was greatest among those who contacted the police via 999. The perception that they were treated impolitely was most common (at 25 per cent) among those who approached an officer in a public place. Although less frequent, complaints about inadequate information and impolite behaviour are things that the police potentially can do something about. Research on crime victims has highlighted the importance they place on being kept informed of what has happened to their case (Shapland and Vagg, 1987; Burrows, 1986; Maguire, 1984; Shapland, 1984; Ekblom and Heal, 1982; Sparks et al., 1977). Among the crime victims who reported their experience to the police, the BCS reveals that fully 56 per cent felt that the police did not keep them adequately informed. The bulk of victims wanted to have been kept better informed, and this lack of communication was strongly related to their dissatisfaction (which was widespread) with how the police handled their case.

Impolite behaviour was the only category other than lack of effort which was linked to social position. The BCS found Afro-Caribbeans were twice as likely as whites to report impolite behaviour by the police. About 10 per cent of whites and Asians with complaints, and 22 per cent of Afro-Caribbeans, indicated that they were not treated politely when they dealt with the police. This is consistent with earlier studies, both in direction and the relative magnitude of ethnic differences (Smith, 1983; Tuck and Southgate, 1981). Impolite behaviour was not a major source of dissatisfaction—Table 5 sets it at about two per cent of all public initiated contacts—but it is also one of the least necessary and perhaps most divisive ones. A more considerate police demeanour is probably the least expensive solution to a problem on this list.

Sources of attitudes

People have a great deal to draw upon besides their own experience when they are making their minds up about the police. The drama of police work, both fact and fiction, commands a great deal of public attention. It is probably the case that the public hears, reads and talks about the police more than any other local public agency. This raises the question of whether people's attitudes towards the police are shaped more by their actual experiences, or by media images which may be less directly connected to the reality of the service they receive. To assess this, participants in the survey were asked how they generally learned about police activities. Those who were interviewed could mention more than one source of information, and most did. For this report, their responses were categorised into four groups. The first—with 32 per cent of all respondents—included people who indicated that they relied on things that they had seen or had happened to them, or that had involved people that they know. A large majority of them had had some recent contact with police. Those who indicated that they got their information from local or national newspapers constituted another group, encompassing 53 per cent of the total. The largest group (59 per cent) were those who relied on radio or television. There were also some respondents (35 per cent) who said they relied on 'just talking to people'. To examine the impact of experiential versus other sources of information on attitudes toward the police, these indicators of people's sources of information were related to their general attitudes (using questions asked of all respondents) and to the satisfaction or dissatisfaction of those who had contacted the police for some reason during the previous 14 months. The analysis also controlled for other determinants of people's attitudes, including age, gender, ethnicity, and education.

The statistical results are summarised in Table B-6, in Appendix B. It indicates that the effect of relying upon direct or indirect experience with the police was about twice as important as either newspapers or the electronic media in shaping people's perceptions of the police. Controlling for many other factors (including their social background, city size, and local housing conditions), those who identified television, radio, and newspapers as their sources of information were more positive in their assessments of police performance (measured by thinking they generally do a 'very good job') and more likely to think police in their area were above average. At the same time, those who relied on their own experiences or the direct experiences of others were generally *less satisfied* with police performance. They gave police lower marks, controlling for many other factors. The negative effect of experience was felt by the general population when asked to rate the quality of police service, and also by those who had contacted the police directly.

An analysis of key sub-groups indicates that the media had the most influence on those who had no recent contacts with the police. Those who had contacted or were stopped by the police, or had been involved in traffic offences, were three times more likely than those with no recent contact to mention their own experiences. When asked if police in their own area were doing a good job or a poor job, people with no recent contact were almost twice as likely as others to say they had no opinion, The media were more influential in rural areas and among older people; city dwellers, young adults, and those with more education tended to rely on their own and others' direct experiences. The force of experience turned out not to be to the advantage of the police, however. Rather, the media seem to cast a generally positive light over police activities, while the sum of people's experiences tended to work in the opposite direction.

Public satisfaction and the limits of policing

The 1988 BCS raises important questions about public opinion and policing. The police have a 'marketing' problem in their apparent indifference in too many situations. This conclusion is in line with past studies of crime victims and others who have come into contact with police. From the consumer's point of view, the willingness of police to assume *responsibility* for dealing as best they can with the problem at hand is their most frequent source of satisfaction or dissatisfaction

19

(Ekblom and Heal, 1982; Sparks *et al.*, 1977). An apparent lack of interest or failure by police to take a complaint seriously signals to the public that they are unwilling to act. This inaction, more frequently than their ability to 'solve' the case in some way, undermines public confidence in them[6]. A pilot survey in Devon and Cornwall (Jones, 1983) suggested that the public looked more to how they were assisted and comforted, and the kindness with which they were treated, than to the ability of police to catch someone; less than a quarter gave reasons for being satisfied that reflected the technical competence or task efficiency of the police. Tuck and Southgate (1981) found that Afro-Caribbeans were twice as dissatisfied with how police treated them 'as a person' as with the actual help that they received. Maguire (1983) recommends that police take this charge seriously. Victims expect police to 'do something', and they should not adopt an officious stance when they feel they cannot. Problems which may appear trivial or routine to police are not necessarily everyday matters to those facing them. A careful reading of reports describing annoyances with police behaviour gathered in the 1982 BCS led Moxon and Jones (1984) to conclude that many incidents about which people were dissatisfied were by some measure trivial, but that their negative reaction could easily have been avoided if officers had been more tactful and sensitive to how those problems looked to complainants.

Maguire suggests that police should not disguise their efforts in this regard. They should be more conspicuous in the pursuit of their duties, letting victims know they are searching for witnesses or evidence, taking careful note of what victims tell them, and giving them the recognition and reassurance they frequently need. In some places police liaison officers make referrals to support groups without victims knowing who passed along their name (Newburn, 1989); it would be helpful if this were instead tied to police efforts at the scene, and that they played a role in assessing the extent and kind of assistance which was required. Unfortunately, this kind of on-scene support runs counter to another (but not the only) trend in policing, towards a crime control stance calling for rapid responses to calls for service, arrests, and other easily measurable indicators of efficiency. This trend has been driven by new police technology, an emerging police professional orientation which emphasises technical proficiency and narrow law enforcement goals, and the adoption of modern management techniques and performance measures (Manning, 1986; Jones, 1983). Reiner (1985) points out that rank and file officers share this disdain for non-crime matters, albeit for different reasons. Jones' (1983) survey of the public and police officers in several regions also found that police overestimated the extent to which the public favoured them on the basis of their technical proficiency and crime fighting success, and underestimated the importance of personalised service in shaping public attitudes.

The 1988 BCS also suggests that, on the other side, public education is called for

---

[6]However, there is evidence (summarised by Box, Hale and Andrews, 1988) that perceived police technical proficiency is linked to reduced fear of crime.

regarding the real role played by the police in responding to crime. As indicated above (in Table 4), the survey found that victims and those who otherwise telephoned police were substantially more satisfied when a meeting with an officer ensued. Table 5 reported that 14 per cent of those who had a specific complaint about police service mentioned that the police did not arrive fast enough, and another 20 per cent were unhappy because the police did not apprehend anyone or recover their lost property. Unfortunately, by these difficult standards, it is not clear that the police *can* improve their ratings very much.

The difficulty is that the police have only a limited capacity for controlling crime. The best evidence is that, beyond the cases with which victims and witnesses can immediately assist them, the police can make arrests and recover property in relatively few instances (Burrows and Tarling, 1987; Hough, 1987; Ekblom and Heal, 1982). Crime is a furtive activity; for example, the vast majority of property thefts do not involve any witnesses or meaningful clues, and simply cannot be solved (Skogan and Antunes, 1979). There is no evidence that the long-term decline in clear-up rates which began in Britain in the early 1970s can do better than stabilise, for it is largely due to factors which are out of the control of the police (including, ironically, increased reporting by victims — see Hough and Mayhew, 1985).

The public's expectation that their complaints will be answered rapidly also poses a great problem for police managers. Other Home Office research has documented that there is a direct trade-off between the time it takes police to get to the scene when they are summoned and the extent of satisfaction among those who summoned them (Ekblom and Heal, 1982). The police can try to meet this expectation, but it is more important that the public develops a realistic view of the costs and benefits of rapid response. In terms of solving crime, the benefits are relatively few (Burrows and Tarling, 1987; Ekblom and Heal, 1982). American research indicates that people's *expectations* with regard to appropriate response times can be altered by describing how police would prefer to deal with their case, and that they are satisfied with reasonable response times when they understand how and when their call will be dealt with (Ekblom and Heal, 1982).

An even more difficult issue is when to send officers to the scene at all. Crime has been increasing at a more rapid rate than police resources, and many police forces have begun to experiment with schemes to match some requests for service with alternative modes of response — for instance, screening out cases after investigations make it evident that there is little hope of their being cleared up. A growing proportion of those who telephone police (but there is as yet no good national estimate of how many) are being given advice or assistance by telephone rather than in person, some are being asked to go to a police station with their problem, and others are finding that they have to wait longer for police to come in response to their telephone call. In the United States, some forces are experimenting with mail-back crime reports, and many more are scheduling next-day responses to requests for service, or are completing case reports entirely over the telephone. These 'graded response' policies are a tactical reaction to mounting police workloads, and they are justified by the largely non-emergency, non-crime character of requests for police service. Evaluations in the United States indicate that they can be very effective at conserving police resources, and that little is lost when a brief screening by telephone indicates that there is minimal chance of clearing up the case. However, this tactic runs counter to public expectations. The 1988 BCS documents the strong, independent effect of satisfaction with the police of meeting complainants. This is in line with previous Home Office research: when presented with alternative ways their cases could have been handled, a sample of people who had telephoned for police assistance overwhelmingly indicated they still preferred that an officer be sent to the scene (Ekblom and Heal, 1982). Jones *et al.,* (1986) found 'immediate response to 999 calls' was the number one policing priority in the Borough of Islington. Although increasingly unrealistic, these expectations are important. Like beliefs concerning response time, they need to be dealt with directly. The 1988 BCS indicates that police are meeting complainants in about 80 per cent of crime calls, but this figure drops off sharply for other kinds of public initiated contacts. It is likely that police will be going to the scene in response to routine matters even less frequently in the future.

Is the public well served?

The last few sections of this chapter have documented that public satisfaction with police service is a function of at least four sets of factors: *who* contacts the police and *where, why* they contact them, and the *nature of the police response.* The police response can be characterised by whether or not they meet those who called at the scene when summoned, the degree of effort they extended in the case, and their personal demeanour. Racial minorities, younger people, males, the unemployed and less educated, and residents of large cities came away less satisfied with the results of these encounters. Likewise, those who contacted police about crime and disturbance problems were less satisfied. The impact of all of these factors is summarised in Figure 1.

As Figure 1 suggests, the relationship *between* the factors summarised in Table 4 could possibly obscure their effects. For example, Afro-Caribbeans and Asians were more likely than whites to telephone the police and visit police stations concerning crime, rather than for other reasons; inner city residents also were much more likely to telephone or visit police stations concerning crime. Younger people were about a third again as likely to contact them about crime as were those over 45, while older people more frequently were concerned about disorder problems. Thus youths, racial minorities, and people living in big cities may be critical of the police on the grounds of how effectively they deal with crime. On the other hand, people tended to give the police higher marks when they actually met them, and, because attendance at the scene was more likely when responding to a crime report, it might be expected that the criticisms of youths, racial minorities etc., would be offset by this effect. However, to complicate things further, what police did at the scene also was related both to who the complainants were and why they telephoned.

Figure 1

Factors shaping satisfaction with police responses

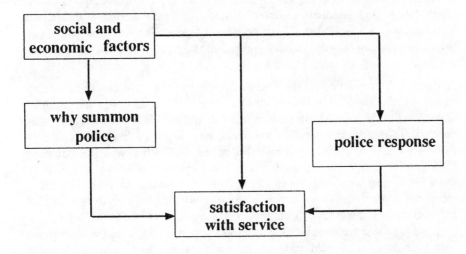

Because of the complex inter-relatedness of these factors, multivariate statistical techniques were employed to take all of them into account at the same time. This analysis was guided by Figure 1. Table B-5, in Appendix B of this report, presents the results of this investigation. It indicates that the main findings suggested by Table 4 hold when many factors are taken into account. Focusing on 999 and police station telephone contacts, the strongest predictors of dissatisfaction were reasons for calling the police, followed by ethnicity. These factors were significant regardless of the type of place where people lived (ranging from inner city to rural area). Whether or not the police met complainants was about as influential as age and gender. Meeting complainants at the scene was largely incident driven; that is, it was strongly influenced by why the police were contacted, and not by much else. Controlling for the type of call and the police response, there still were independent effects of social and economic factors on people's satisfaction with the service they received.

As this suggests, the overall impact of the service rendered by the police in these public initiated encounters was not clearly in their favour. A large majority of those who contacted the police were satisfied with the service they received, but there was an erosion of support among some of those who relied upon them. The largest gaps were between the races. Among those who had not contacted the police over the past 14 months, 13 per cent of whites, 16 per cent of Afro-Caribbeans, and 16 per cent of Asians thought they were doing a poor or very poor job; as these figures are based on samples, there is essentially no difference between them. On the other hand, among those who had telephoned or gone to the police, 14 per cent of whites, 31 per cent of Afro-Caribbeans, and 31 per cent of Asians gave them low marks. These differences are very large, and suggest that the aggregate effects of why they contacted the police, the police response, and character of their encounters, were divisive in nature. A similar, albeit less dramatic erosion of support can be found in other groups, including males, the unemployed, and residents of council housing. There were few differences between those who did and did not contact the police in rural areas and small towns, but the gap between the two grew a little larger in metropolitan and inner city areas.

A significant proportion of the overall decline in support for police overtime which was documented at the outset of this report is attributable to mounting dissatisfaction among those who contacted the police. Crime victims were decidedly less satisfied with police performance in 1988 than they were in the 1984 BCS. Among victims who reported to the police, satisfaction was down in many demographic categories and for virtually every category of crime. It was down more for victims who made reports than it was for those who did not report to the police. The proportion of victims who were very satisfied with the service they received declined by nine percentage points between 1984 and 1988. Satisfaction declined the most among older victims and manual workers, and was down for both sexes, in all socio-economic groups, and for home owners, private tenants, and residents of council housing. The proportion of victims dissatisfied because the police 'didn't do enough', rose by ten percentage points. The proportion of victims who said they were dissatisfied because police failed to keep them informed about their case grew from 21 to 34 per cent. (For more details on these 1984-88 changes, see Mayhew, Elliott, and Dowds, 1989.)

The fact that support for the police diminishes with the actual need for their services, and is going down substantially among their main 'customers'— crime victims — presents them with a very great challenge. The mass media appear to cast a rather positive aura over police activities, and police seem to smoothly share routine information with the public. This is important, for Neighbourhood Watch and new community policing initiatives promise to increase the volume of informal, information-sharing encounters between police and the general public. The increased involvement of the public in routine policing hopefully will encourage their trust and support, enable communities to articulate their views and expectations with regard to policing more clearly, and enable the police to do a better job (Jones, 1983).

However, when the focus shifts from these largely discretionary police-public contacts to those which are more event-driven, including telephone calls to the police concerning crime and disturbance problems, dissatisfaction is more manifest. More client dissatisfaction is associated with activities which lie at the heart of the traditional police function. We do not know the effect of this on their *future* co-operation with the police (measured by their willingness to contact them again, and to co-operate further in their investigations), but the sum of these experiences may undermine police effectiveness. Further, the sum of these contacts appears to be racially divisive; Asians and Afro-Caribbeans who came into contact with the police stood further from the white majority at the end of the day than those who did not.

3 Policing the Public

While the previous chapter focused on serving the public, this one examines policing the public. It is the duty of the police to seek out infractions of the law through routine patrols and special investigations, and among the powers at their disposal are those to stop people or vehicles, and conduct searches. Since the last BCS was conducted, stop and search powers have been affected by the Police and Criminal Evidence Act of 1984. Previously, the police did not possess a general power to stop and search for stolen goods or prohibited articles, although a variety of local powers existed. PACE consolidated many of those local provisions and police now have a uniform statutory authority to stop persons or vehicles on the reasonable suspicion that they would find stolen goods or prohibited articles. PACE also requires that a written record be made of searches attendant to these stops. These provisions came into effect at the beginning of 1986. There are also a number of grounds for stopping persons or vehicles contained in other legislation; for example, to search for controlled drugs, or to see the licences and insurance certificates of anyone operating a motor vehicle.

To examine the enforcement of these provisions, the BCS asked about street encounters involving people when they were either driving or out walking. This is far from a full account for police initiated activity. It ignores the more exotic and exciting aspects of police work portrayed in television fiction and news programmes, and it overlooks many routine police duties. Nonetheless, street encounters are one of the primary points of contact between ordinary people and the police. They differ from those examined earlier in several respects. They are imposed on the public, rather than by them; they imply at least some suspicion by the police that their target is up to no good; and they are potentially abrasive or even violent. The need for fair and lawful treatment of suspected persons, an even-handed approach to dealing with people of different backgrounds, and a professional demeanour on the part of police officers, are also issues in these cases. These requirements are not unique to police initiated encounters with the public, but they are more problematic in the case of street stops.

This section examines the distribution of proactive street activity, some important details concerning what happened during the course of these encounters, and how people feel they were treated by the police. The laws and rules of procedure applicable to stops and searches have changed somewhat since the last comparable BCS survey of public encounters with police, so this section also examines changes in patterns of street enforcement since then. Surveys like the BCS are probably the only useful measures of the frequency of street encounters, for they suggest that a large majority of them slip through official record keeping procedures. These encounters are again described from the point of view of their civilian participants. In this case they were the targets, rather than consumers of policing, and this doubtless coloured their views of what happened. This is particularly likely to be true when they were asked how they were treated by police, and in that light the fact that three-quarters or more thought they were dealt with appropriately is heartening. However, these stops and searches also had measurable negative consequences; a significant number of those caught up in them were unhappy about how they were treated, and their effects were racially divisive.

Who gets stopped?

BCS respondents were asked if, in the past 14 months (including all of 1987 and early 1988), they had been in a car or on a motorcycle ' ... which was approached or stopped by police officers because they thought an offence had been committed?' If the answer was 'yes', there followed a series of questions about the reasons for the stop, if anyone was searched, if the police were polite or not, and about various traffic tickets, breath tests, notices, and warnings they might have received. About 75 per cent of these incidents involved possible traffic offences. The report will refer to these as 'traffic stops'. Participants in the BCS were also asked if they had been 'stopped and asked questions by the police' whilst they were on foot, and similar follow-up questions were asked of those who indicated that they had. These will be referred to as pedestrian encounters in the remainder of this report. It is important to note that — unlike traffic stops — the question probing the incidence of pedestrian encounters did not specify that a potential offence was involved. Other kinds of encounters, perhaps involving warnings concerning untoward but not criminal behaviour, police requests for information, or attempts on their part to make their presence visible in order to help maintain order, could well account for some of these situations.

In addition, a 'clean-up' question in the BCS asked about contacts with the police which were not otherwise discussed and a number of the encounters described there fall into the police initiated contact category. These included being 'told to move on' and police visits 'to search your house'. These were combined into an 'other' category. In many respects they closely resembled pedestrian stops (see table B–7), but their small number and heterogeneous character precluded doing much with them in the analyses presented here. Stops in this category are included in Table 6, but otherwise are not examined in the main body of the report.

In light of the large volume of traffic summonses issued each year, it should be no surprise that a large number of those interviewed (about 736 in the combined sample of 6297 respondents) had been involved in traffic stops. A substantially smaller number were involved in police initiated pedestrian encounters (only 174 in the combined sample), which will limit the inferences that can be made about them from the data. Overall, the best estimate by the BCS is that about three per cent of the residents of England and Wales were involved in pedestrian encounters during 1987 and early 1988, and about 12 per cent were involved in traffic stops. There was some overlap between the two categories: about one quarter of those stopped on foot were involved in a traffic stop, whilst 6 per cent of those involved in a vehicle stop were also stopped while on foot.

Table 6 .

Groups stopped by the police

Group	Per cent stopped	(N)	Group	Per cent stopped	(N)
RACE			OCCUPATION	*	
whites	15	(4642)	semi/unskilled	13	(989)
Afro-Caribbeans	20 **	(510)	skilled manual	13	(1380)
Asians	14	(748)	non-managerial	16	(853)
			professional	18	(1393)
AGE	**			*	
16-24	35	(723)	council housing	12	(1063)
25-29	19	(407)	all others	16	(3797)
30-44	16	(1293)			
45-59	12	(1145)	inner city	15	(847)
60 plus	4	(1272)	metropolitan	15	(1044)
			urbanised areas	15	(927)
INCOME	**		mixed areas	18	(1090)
under £10,000	9	(1796)	rural areas	13	(957)
£10-£20,000	15	(1176)			
£20,000 or more	21	(615)	LEFT SCHOOL	**	
			under age 15	6	(1172)
GENDER	**		all others	18	(3644)
males	20	(2342)			
females	10	(2523)	MARITAL STATUS	**	
			never married	29	(1010)
VEHICLE ACCESS	**		all others	12	(3845)
have access	18	(3750)			
no access	7	(1115)	EMPLOYMENT STATUS	**	
			unemployed	22	(574)
			all others	14	(4292)
ALL RESPONDENTS	15	(4866)			

Weighted data. ** indicates significant multivariate relationship for a variable controlling for other factors in the table; * indicates a significant bivariate relationship. For a detailed analysis by type of contact, see Table B–7.

Table 6 describes the distribution of those contacts, combining both traffic and pedestrian stops. As in Table 1, it was useful to combine them because they were related in similar fashion to many other factors. Differences between the two kinds of street encounters were largely confined to age (pedestrian encounters drop off sharply after age 25), and income (which is only related to traffic stops, through vehicle ownership). Table B–7 in Appendix B presents separate demographic breakdowns for each kind of stop.

Topping the list in Table 6 were young adults between 16 and 24 years of age; more than one third of them recalled being stopped by the police in a 14 month period. Others near the top were single people and the unemployed, and upper income respondents. The latter is primarily due to automobile ownership, which is also included in Table 6. Males and Afro-Caribbeans round out the list of groups near the top in terms of their risk of being stopped by the police; there was no difference between Asians and whites in this response. These patterns closely resemble the distribution of police initiated contacts revealed by the Policy Studies Institute's survey of London in 1981 (Smith, 1983).

The categories reported in Table 6 both overlap one another and sometimes accumulate in their effects. For example, combining gender and age, a full 48 per cent of all young males interviewed in the BCS recalled being involved in a street stop in 1987 and early 1988. The comparable figure for young, Afro-Caribbean males was 56 per cent. The effects of the various factors in Table 6 can also cancel one another. Afro-Caribbeans are more likely to be younger, unemployed, and unmarried — all factors related to the frequency with which people are stopped by the police. On the other hand, they are *less* likely to have direct access to a motor vehicle and less often come from higher-income households, factors which are related to being involved in traffic stops.

Controlling for vehicle ownership causes the apparently positive association between income and the risk of being stopped by the police to disappear (see Table B–8 in Appendix B). Occupational status, and social class, (which is not shown here) were also linked to contact with the police through vehicle ownership. However, the remaining factors shown in Table 6 were independently related to being stopped by police, including the fact that Asians were less likely than others to be stopped by the police.

In addition to these basic social and economic factors, the current life styles and recent activities of people are also linked to their risk of being stopped by police. A few of these factors are summarised in Table 7. Not surprisingly, those who had driven great distances during 1987 were much more likely than others to have been involved in traffic stops. In addition, respondents who report that they go out frequently during the evening were more likely to be caught up in both pedestrian and traffic encounters. There also was a tendency for people who had been in trouble with the police in the past to get into trouble again. BCS respondents were questioned briefly about their previous brushes with the law. By this measure, those with a criminal record had a high risk of being stopped again by the police; among those involved in a pedestrian encounter, fully 15 per cent reported that they had been arrested prior to 1987, the year covered by the survey. The comparable figure for those involved in traffic stops was 11 per cent,

29

but only four per cent of those who were not stopped by the police in 1987 recalled being arrested before then.

Table 7

Lifestyle factors and stops by police

Category	Traffic stop	Pedestrian encounter	Both stops	(N)
EVENINGS OUT				
PER WEEK	**	**	**	
0	5	1	8	(1719)
1	9	2	12	(1034)
2	13	3	17	(729)
3–4	18	4	23	(787)
5–7	24	7	30	(559)
MILES DRIVEN				
IN LAST YEAR	**		**	
none/no vehicle	5	2	9	(1819)
under 5,000	9	3	12	(1065)
5000–14,999	16	2	19	(1489)
15,000 or more	30	2	32	(505)
PAST ARRESTS	**	**	**	
arrest in 5 yrs.	23	8	31	(264)
not arrested	11	2	14	(4592)
ALL RESPONDENTS	12	3	15	(4865)

Weighted data. ** indicates significant multivariate relationship controlling for the other variables in this table *and* the demographic factors listed in Table 6. For the multivariate analysis, see Table B-8.

Almost all the relationships in Table 7 were significant, controlling for the demographic factors described above, despite the fact that they were closely interrelated (this is documented in Table B-8). Multivariate analyses suggest that the low level of Asian involvement in street encounters is explained in part by their limited exposure to risk of being stopped (fewer miles driven; fewer evenings out per week) and lower likelihood of having a history of past arrests.[1] Higher status people reported driving longer distances, and males were more likely to report driving and being out at night, and measures of those activities explained most of their higher risk of being stopped. Factors which were not measured in the 1988 BCS doubtless played an important role as well. The role of alcohol was examined in the 1982 BCS, and self reports of typical alcohol consumption were

[1]For a discussion of interpreting 'control' factors, see Appendix A.

strongly related to the risk of being involved in both traffic and pedestrian stops (Southgate and Ekblom, 1984).

A clear picture emerges from the factors examined here: the police are more likely to stop and question young, single, unemployed, Afro-Caribbean males. Having a record of past criminal encounters with police also put one at substantially greater risk of being stopped, as did going out frequently at night and driving a great deal. In turn, the impact of other factors on the risk of being stopped is independent of this measure of past involement with the police.

Repeated stops

The BCS indicates that overall, about 15 per cent of the residents of England and Wales were stopped by the police during 1987 and early 1988. The number of *persons* involved did not coincide with the number of pedestrian or traffic *stops* made by police, of course, for some are caught up in these investigations more than once. The BCS indicates that the impact of the relatively small number of persons who are repeatedly stopped on the total number of stops made by police is quite large.

Most of those involved in police initiated investigations were stopped only once or twice; they accounted for 86 per cent of all persons involved in pedestrian encounters; and 89 per cent of those caught up in traffic stops. However, the remaining 14 per cent of BCS respondents involved in multiple pedestrian encounters accounted for *45 per cent* of all stops. Traffic stops were somewhat less repetitive, but the 11 per cent of those who were stopped frequently, accounted for 34 per cent of the total[2].

A profile of the persons involved in multiple stops is presented in Table 8. As before, it is useful to combine traffic and pedestrian situations because the two groups were similar. Unlike the Policey Studies Institute's London survey (Smith, 1983), the 1988 BCS does *not* point to significant differences (given the sample sizes) between whites and Afro-Caribbeans in the frequence with which they are caught up in multiple encounters with the police. Tuck and Southgate (1981) came to the same conclusion in their study of Manchester. Asians, on the other hand, were distinctly less likely than others to be stopped three times or more, and this difference remained very large when the other factors were taken into account. Males, young adults, and people with lower-status occupations were more likely to be involved in traffic or pedestrian stops on a repetitive basis. Table 8 indicates that whether or not these respondents had access to a household motor vehicle (which was related to being involved in vehicle stops as either a passenger or driver) was not very related to repetitive stops, and its effect disappeared when other factors were taken into account. There also were no real differences in the rate of multiple stops in the inner cities as opposed to other

---

[2] These are conservative estimates, employing the lowest point in the '6-9 times' response category used in BCS questions concerning the frequency of police initiated contacts, and assigning all persons stopped '10 or more times' a value of 10.

places, for residents of council housing, or even when self-reports of past arrests are taken into account.

Table 8

Repeated stops by police

Group	Number of people stopped more than once as a percentage of people stopped once or more	(N)
RACE		
whites	12	(630)
Afro-Caribbeans	19	(96)
Asians	6**	(100)
AGE	**	
16 - 24	19	(241)
25 - 29	15	(75)
30 plus	7	(347)
GENDER		
males	16**	(442)
females	4	(223)
OCCUPATIONAL STATUS		
manual	18**	(274)
non-manual	9	(358)
ACCESS TO A VEHICLE		
no	9	(61)
yes	13	(604)
ALL RESPONDENTS	12	(665)

Weighted data. ** indicates significant controlling for other factors. For the multi-variate analysis, see Table B-8.

The exercise of discretion

One of the most interesting features of these traffic and pedestrian encounters is that little that was serious seemed to come of most of them. Of those who were stopped on foot, only four per cent reported being arrested, and three per cent were prosecuted. Although some people may be reluctant to admit an arrest or prosecution to interviewers, the figures are in fact almost identical to Willis's (1983) earlier estimate for the UK as a whole, and to the Merseyside crime survey (Kinsey, 1985). The comparable figures for those involved in traffic stops were one per cent arrested and 10 per cent prosecuted; there were more prosecutions than arrests in the traffic-stop category because the most common sanctions dispensed by police in those instances were fixed penalty and vehicle defect notices.[3] Taking a very broad definition of 'official action', including arrests,

---

[3]Respondents who were involved in traffic stops as passengers are classified here by what happened to their drivers.

receiving penalty and vehicle notices, being asked to take a breath test, statements by police that they 'would' be summonsed, and just having their names taken, only one quarter of those involved in traffic stops, and less than 15 per cent of those stopped while on foot, were officially sanctioned in any way. The remainder received warnings or advice, or were just questioned.

One result of this low level sanctioning is that most of these police initiated encounters with the public had no continuing legal consequences. By this measure they were not very adversarial. However, they are also evidence of just how highly discretionary police actions on the street can be. Some of the circumstances that trigger street stops lead to almost automatic police action. An encounter in which a vehicle proved to be unsafe or the driver appeared to be drunk would call for a defect notice or a breath test; the discovery of weapons, drugs, or contraband would spark an arrest. However, based on what the police *did,* only a portion of these street stops — just over 20 per cent involved something warranting a sanction by even a very broad standard, and only a very small percentage led to an arrest. Instead, the police were exercising a great deal of discretion in a substantial number of cases stopping and questioning people, and then letting them go without taking any action. This low-level, low-visibility policing of the public, which takes place on a day by day basis, constituted the bulk of police initiated contacts with the public.

One great concern is that the widespread exercise of discretionary authority by officials of all kinds can lead to abuses, or to at least the feeling by some that they are being harassed. The BCS cannot examine this issue directly, for it has no independent measures of what people were doing when they were stopped which may have attracted attention. However, a more sensitive indicator of how people are treated may be found in their reports of what happened once they were stopped. One police action which was identified in the BCS was whether or not they were *searched.* A small but important portion of those involved in these encounters were searched; 10 per cent of vehicles or drivers, and 22 per cent of those stopped on foot.

Searches outside the police station are highly discretionary police tactics, and might well provoke concern or even hostility from those searched. The BCS probably provides the best estimate of their frequency and distribution. Unless street encounters generate a summons, an arrest, or some other tangible record that they took place, systematic knowledge of their occurrence is hard to come by. The 1981 Policy Studies Institute survey of Londoners found that in about 60 per cent of all street stops, people did not recall having their names or addresses taken, and the police apparently made no formal record that these stops had taken place (Smith, 1983). The 1988 BCS did not ask about stops in this much detail. The Police and Criminal Evidence Act of 1984 was designed to formalise stop and search procedures throughout the country, and requires all stops that involve searches to be recorded. A later section on the effects of PACE compares the figures on stop and search from previous sweeps of the BCS with official statistics[4].

Table 9 summarises the distribution of street searches reported in the BCS. It resembles that of other police initiated actions. Afro-Caribbeans, youths, males, the unemployed, and residents of areas BCS interviewers judged to have bad housing, were all more frequently searched once they were stopped. Table 9 also shows that these contrasts persisted after controlling for other factors.

Table 9

The exercise of direction by police

Group	Traffic stops per cent searched	(N)	Pedestrian encounters per cent searched	(N)
RACE whites	9	(531)	20	(131)
Afro-Carribeans	34**	(82)	36	(24)
Asians	14	(71)	25	(13)
AGE	**		*	
16-24	17	(192)	31	(73)
older	7	(368)	12	(65)
GENDER	**		**	
males	12	(369)	28	(104)
females	7	(195)	4	(32)
AREA HOUSING	**		**	
rated fair/bad	15	(180)	30	(55)
rated good	7	(369)	18	(76)
HOUSING TENURE	*			
Council	16	(98)	26	(39)
all others	9	(468)	21	(98)
EMPLOYMENT STATUS			**	
unemployed	21	(89)	46	(41)
all others	8	(474)	12	(95)
PAST ARRESTS	**		**	
arrest 5 years	18	(61)	35	(21)
not arrested	9	(473)	15	(102)
ALL RESPONDENTS	10	(563)	22	(137)

Weight data. ** indicates significant multivariate relationship controlling for other factors in the table; * indicates a significant bivariate relationship. For the multivariate analysis, see Table B-9.

---

[4]Searches in traffic stops were not very productive. In fact, not one case in the BCS sample involving a search ended in arrest, and non-search cases lead to slightly more sanctions than cases in which drivers or vehicles were searched. This is quite different from the pattern revealed by official reports of searches and arrests; Home Office Statistical Bulletin (1989) indicates that one in six searches is linked to an arrest, while in the 1988 BCS it was one in seventeen.

Table 9 also documents how those who admitted being arrested before are more likely to attract the close attention of the police. The inclusion of this measure serves to subtract this source of police wariness from the multivariate effects of the other factors summarised in Table 9.

Both of the discretionary decisions by the police to stop and search, place them in potentially abrasive encounters with people on the street. It is also important to note that there is no evidence of widespread abuse of police authority in the limited data on street stops collected by the BCS. In over 90 per cent of traffic and 80 per cent of pedestrian encounters, those who were involved indicated that they were given a reason for being stopped. In both cases, well over 80 per cent of people given a reason indicated that it was a good one. In a large majority of pedestrian searches those involved were given reasons for being searched; when they were, most judged that it was 'a good enough reason' (those who were caught up in traffic stops were not asked this question). However, to the extent that these encounters have effects on the attitudes and future co-operativeness of those concerned, this low level policing can have divisive consequences. A later section of this chapter illustrates that this has been the case.

Reactions to stops

It is clear that those who are stopped, either on foot or on the road, are less happy about the police as a result. 21 per cent thought the police generally do a 'poor job' or a 'fairly poor job' as against 12 per cent of people who had not been stopped. They were also three times as likely to think that police service in their area was worse than in other places. Dissatisfaction among those caught up in street stops has also increased over time, accounting for some of the decline in confidence in police noted in the first section of this report. Taking as a measure the proportion saying that police do a 'very good job', confidence dropped very sharply between 1982 and 1988 (from 33 per cent to only 18 per cent) among people involved in traffic stops, and it was also down (but not significantly, given the small numbers) from 28 to 23 per cent among those stopped while on foot.

One reason for dissatisfaction was that some who were stopped by the police did not feel they were well treated. They were decidedly not in the majority, but about one quarter of those stopped by the police while on foot, and about one in five of those involved in a traffic stop, rated the police as 'a bit' or 'very impolite'.

Table 10 summarises responses to a question in the BCS concerning how politely respondents were treated by police. People's experiences with the police were segmented by age, race, and place of residence. Older people who were stopped by the police were more likely to recall that they were treated politely, as were whites. There was a tendency for residents of small towns and rural areas to report more satisfactory experiences of the police. Differences between the experiences of those who had a past record of arrest and those who did not were not statistically significant.

35

Table 10

Reactions of persons stopped by the police

Group	Traffic stops per cent very polite	(N)	Pedestrian encounters per cent very polite	(N)
RACE				
whites	48	(513)	51	(130)
Afro Caribbeans	24**	(78)	12**	(23)
Asians	31**	(86)	50	(13)
AGE				
16-24	34**	(188)	35**	(71)
older	54	(358)	67	(63)
AREA				
inner/metro	43**	(205)	46	(58)
urban areas	44	(101)	60	(30)
mixed/rural	51	(239)	48	(46)
SEARCH				
search	24**	(55)	11**	(30)
no search	49	(490)	61	(104)
SANCTIONS				
sanction	38**	(136)	17**	(18)
no sanction	50	(410)	55	(116)
REASON FOR STOP				
reason given	48**	(511)	60**	(106)
no reason given	27	(35)	14	(28)
PAST ARRESTS				
past arrest	40	(59)	37	(21)
no arrests	48	(481)	52	(113)
ALL RESPONDENTS	47	(545)	50	(134)

Weighted data. ** indicates significant multivariate relationship controlling for other factors in the table; * indicates a significant bivariate relationship.

It could be argued that the reactions of people to encounters like this are determined mainly by whether or not they worked their way out of them without being arrested, issued a summons, or having their name taken. The dissatisfied may just be those who got 'nicked'.

The 1988 sweep of the BCS indicates that this is true. Table 10 shows consistent differences between those who were sanctioned (eg. issued a summons or a penalty notice, given a breath test or a defect notice, or arrested) and those who were not. As in Smith's (1983) London survey, persons involved in street stops who were not sanctioned had a more favourable view of how they were treated; conversely, those who were searched were less pleased. However, an important determinant of how people thought they were treated was police procedure. How they were dealt with counted, as well as whether or not they were penalised. This can be seen in Table 10 under the effects of giving reasons to people when they are stopped on the street. The apparently salutary effect of this simple courtesy is in line with a great deal of research (summarised in Tyler and Lind, 1988) that suggests that the even-handedness and openness with which people are treated by government (their sense that they got 'procedural justice') often outweighs in importance whether or not a decision eventually goes their way. In this case, simple indicators of whether or not police *explained why* they made stops overshadowed the extent to which people were searched or sanctioned in determining their assessments of how they were treated.

We saw previously that there also was a pattern to people's assessments of how they were treated during these encounters. Youths, racial minorities, and males more often reported that they were treated impolitely, and were less positive about police performance. Some — but not all — of those differences are explained by the ways in which their cases were handled. Women and older people were less likely to be sanctioned, and women were more likely to be told why they were stopped. Unemployed persons and those from the lowest status groups were more likely to be sanctioned and less likely to be given reasons why they were stopped. Afro-Caribbeans were significantly less likely than either whites or Asians to be told why they were stopped, either in traffic or pedestrian stops. These partially confounding effects are clarified to a certain degree by a multivariate analysis which is summarised in Table 10. It illustrates the independent importance of both negative (searches; sanctioning) and positive (reasons) elements of the situation, plus the continuing effects of race, age, and inner city location, on how people felt they were treated during these encounters.

Official complaints against police

In addition to assessing people's general reactions to police, the BCS also asked whether or not they had attempted to lodge a formal complaint concerning police behaviour. This is a relatively infrequent occurrence, so for this topic the survey shifted its focus from the recent past to a period of the past five years. Still, only a few respondents recalled making a formal complaint.

Participants in the BCS were first asked if they had been 'really annoyed' about the way a police officer had behaved toward them or someone they knew, or about how police had handled a case in which they were involved. When questioned in this broad fashion, about 20 per cent of all BCS respondents recalled being really annoyed during the past five years about some specific police action. About half of these actions involved the respondents themselves, whilst the other half involved someone they knew[5].

Of the 20 per cent who recalled some annoyance, almost exactly half indicated that they felt strongly enough about it to make an official complaint. However, only one in five actually did so. The major reasons given for *not* making a complaint were that it would be ineffective, that complaints would not be taken seriously, and that police would not investigate themselves effectively. Together, these accounted for 31 per cent of cases which were not advanced to the formal complaint stage. There were many scattered reasons why the remainder of these potential complaints were not pursued. About eight indicated they were afraid of doing so, that they did not want to be marked as a troublemaker, or that making a complaint would just make their predicament worse. Another ten per cent reported that they just do not like to complain, did not want to get involved, never got around to it, or characterised themselves as too lazy to do anything about their experience.

In the end, about 1·9 per cent of those who were interviewed had actually made, or tried to make, an official complaint concerning police behaviour[6]. What the complaints were about is described in the second column of Table 11. It classifies complaints into two major groupings: those involving rude, unjustified, excessively forceful, or racist behaviour (dubbed 'poor demeanour' in Table 11), and those relating to inadequate, ineffective, or incompetent police performance in the field ('bad performance'). The inevitable category for 'other' responses (some of which were simply too vague to be classifiable) is presented there as well. The complaints could involve more than one issue, and some did, so the percentages presented in Table 11 total more than 100 per cent. The complaints are summarised by major category, as well as by detailed (and sometimes overlapping) sub-categories.

Table 11 indicates that the bulk of formal complaints regarding the police concerned their demeanour. These complaints most frequently involved the perception that the police had been overbearing, arrogant, unfriendly, or unduly informal in their dealings with people. Perceptions that they had been unjustly stopped or accused were also common among those with complaints. There were fewer complaints concerning the use of excessive force or racist language. Another one third of those with complaints focused on how the police performed their tasks. The largest group of complainants in this category were just upset that the police had done nothing to help them, had not adequately investigated their case, or had failed to give them appropriate help, support, or advice.

---

[5]Moxon and Jones (1984) present a detailed description of the substance of annoyances based on the actual narrative reports gathered in the 1982 BCS, not just on summary classifications of each incident.

[6]In the BCS for 1981, 1·4 per cent of those interviewed indicated they had made an official complaint about something that had happened to them *personally:* the complaint figure for personal experiences in 1987 was 1·3 per cent. The figure given in the text (1·9 per cent) includes complaints concerning police actions against other people as well as against the respondent.

There were not great differences in the content of actual complaints and the things that more generally annoyed people about the police. The distribution of the general annoyances from which official complaints were drawn is presented in the first column of Table 11. Both groups were about equally likely to be concerned about police demeanour or performance issues.

Table 11

Official complaints against police

Nature of complaint	Per cent of persons who were annoyed	Per cent of persons who made a complaint
POOR DEMEANOUR	61	58
—rude, arrogant, overbearing, unfriendly	36	27
—stop or accusation unjustified	21	24
—used undue force	10	16
—racist language or behaviour	1	1
BAD PERFORMANCE	31	37
—inaction; failure to help	15	20
—incompetent or inappropriate action	8	8
—procedural irregularities	5	9
—slow response; police did not come	3	3
—poor follow up; did not keep informed	2	1
—offender not caught; property not recovered	1	1
OTHER OR TOO VAGUE	13	15
—number of respondents	838	92
—number of complaints	968	115

Weighted data. Note that respondents could make more than one complaint, so the percentages sum to more than 100 per cent. The figures for the major categories account for overlaps in complaints within their subcategories.

There generally were no differences between those who were annoyed and those who actually complained on other dimensions; the demographic profile of actual complainants closely fits that of the larger group of persons reporting annoying circumstance.

Both annoyances and complaints were most clearly related to ethnicity. Afro-Caribbeans were *much* more likely than whites or Asians to have been annoyed; 46 per cent of them, as compared to 29 per cent of whites and 22 per cent of Asians, were likely to have had such an experience. However, there were *no* significant differences between the races in terms of actually having made a complaint: only about 10 per cent of those in each ethnic category who had been annoyed reported that they had done so. The relationship between experiencing a felt injustice and actually complaining about it thus differed considerably from group to group, with Afro-Caribbeans being the least likely to follow through with them. This is partly consistent with the Islington Crime Survey; Jones *et al.*, (1986) found both Afro-Caribbeans and Asians were more likely to indicate, when asked about a hypothetical situation, that they would not follow through a complaint.

The groups also differed in *what* annoyed them. Not surprisingly, complaints concerning racist behaviour were confined to Afro-Caribbeans and Asians. Afro-Caribbeans were far more likely than the others to be annoyed about unjustified stops, but less likely to complain about them. They were least likely (by far) to feel that police did not help them or were not concerned about their case. Smith (1983) also found that Afro-Caribbean victims more frequently reported that the police took action, made a full investigation, and caught the offender. He hypothesised that police put full effort into cases involving Afro-Caribbean victims because they feared a complaint otherwise, but the BCS indicates that in fact Afro-Caribbeans are the least likely to proceed with a complaint.

The BCS is unsuited for saying much about the fate of complaints lodged against police, for so few respondents were involved. In addition, the great similarity between the nature of complaints and annoyances, and between respondents who fell in the two groups, suggests it is important to look elsewhere to understand the process by which annoyances become complaints. Part of the problem is doubtless that many people do not understand how complaint procedures work (Brown, 1988). It is also likely that this process is influenced more by how the police treat complaints. Whether grievances are registered or not probably depends upon how well the procedures for making complaints function, the openness or hostility with which they appear to be received, and whether attempts to redress wrongs are made gracefully or grudgingly. There are doubtless also differences from area to area in how grievances are informally resolved without evoking the formal complaint process. One purpose of PACE reforms in the complaints procedure was to enable minor grievances to be cleared up easily and quickly, and without the threat of disciplinary action against individual officers hanging over every case (Brown, 1988).

The effects of PACE

One issue which can be addressed (in part) by the 1988 BCS is the effect of the Police and Criminal Evidence Act of 1984 on police enforcement activity. The findings of the 1988 BCS can be contrasted with those from sweeps of the BCS conducted prior to the enactment of PACE, to discover if there have been any significant shifts in police activity which might be attributable to the new legislation and rules of police practice.

40

There are contradictory expectations with regard to the effects of PACE on street-level enforcement in England and Wales. On the one hand, some police forces did not have general legal authority to make stops and searches before the enactment of PACE, and they may now be making frequent use of it. The expansion of police authority over disorderly conduct authorised by the Public Order Act 1986 might also have increased the volume of street encounters. Recent.offical statistics (which unfortunately do not go back before PACE) point to an increasing use of searches; between 1986 (the first year of PACE) and 1988, they went up almost 50 per cent, principally in London (Home Office Statistical Bulletin, 1989).

On the other hand, PACE superseded an assortment of local rules which already allowed police to make stops and searches. In other areas without such powers the new statute may have formalised unofficial practice. This would lead us to expect few actual (as opposed to officially recorded) changes in police activity. Maguire (1988) refers to the 'mountain of paperwork' generated by PACE for police, and suggests that this might dampen enthusiasm for any new powers it gives them. The establishment of a Crown Prosecution Service under the Prosecution of Offenders Act of 1985 might have led to a *reducing* of the number of prosecutions for some types of offence; the emphasis that the police give to enforcement in those situations may be reduced as a consequence. Finally, the new code of police practice which came along with PACE sets a very high standard of suspicion for making street searches, a level equal to that required to make a arrest. This might tend to *reduce* the level of stop and search in the post-PACE era.

Comparisons of the 1988 BCS with surveys conducted before the passage of PACE suggest that there has been no significant change in police enforcement patterns over the period. In fact, the 1982 and 1988 sweeps of the survey point to a small (statistically insignificant) reduction in the use of powers of stop and search. In the 1982 BCS, 3·2 per cent of those interviewed recalled being stopped while on foot; in the 1988 survey it was 2·8 per cent. In 1982 and 1988, an identical 11·5 indicated they had been caught up in a traffic stop. The proportion of traffic stops in which someone was searched was 13 per cent in the 1982 BCS, and per cent in 1988. Among those involved in pedestrain encounters in 1982, 29 per cent were searched; in 1988 the comparable figure was 22 per cent. Given the sample sizes involved, none of these differences were statistically reliable. Similar contrasts can be made for London, using the 1981 survey conducted there by the Policy Studies Institute (Smith, 1983). It found that 14 per cent of Londoners had been involved in a vehicle stop in the previous 12 months, and three per cent in pedestrian encounters. The comparable figures for London residents included in the 1988 BCS were 11 per cent for traffic stops and three per cent for stops on foot. Like the national figure, none of these small changes in police tactics (as perceived by those on the other side of the exchange) is large enough to point to any trend. They are far from a definitive test of the effects of PACE, but they suggest that there has been a great deal of stability in police operations pre-and post-PACE.

Are they adversaries?

The 1988 BCS reveals that in a 14-month period the police stopped and questioned almost 15 per cent of the adult population. This percentage appears to have remained the same for much of the 1980s. Few of these stops seems to have been sparked by situations which clearly called for an arrest, summons, or some sanction. In about one in five of these encounters the police searched the individuals or vehicles involved, but even the majority of these cases did not lead to offical action. These stops and searches also were related to the social and economic backgrounds of their targets, and they had some measurable consequences. Those who were caught up in them were more likely to rate police service as poor rather than good, and they reported a significant measure of apparently impolite behaviour on the part of the police. On the other hand, there was also evidence that attempts at openness by the police in their dealings with people during street stops paid some dividends.

Figure 2

Factors shaping reactions to street stops

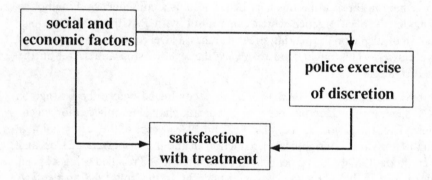

It is common to label police initiated encounters like these as 'adversarial' contacts with the public. They are imposed rather than sought, and they imply at least some level of suspicion that the targets of police investigations were up to no good. However, the BCS indicates the assumption that many of these contacts result in real friction between police and the public may be an overstatement. Rather, the picture that emerges is one of relatively good humour on both sides of the encounter. The factors that were related to dissatisfaction were important, but they were present in only a minority of cases. Relatively few of these encounters had enduring legal consequences. In the overwhelming majority of cases members of the public were told why they were stopped and agreed that the reason was a good one. Those who were searched during these encounters were not as satisfied with how they were treated, but they were far from numerous and a large majority of them also were given what they considered to be good reasons for being stopped. In the end, 82 per cent of those involved in traffic stops and 72 per cent in pedestrian encounters judged that the officer was 'very polite' or 'fairly polite' in their case.

There remains the difficult issue of balancing the benefits of stop and search procedures (the detection of criminals and the prevention of crime) against the ill effects of worsening relationships between the police and the community. This problem is apparent in the social distribution of street stops. Young, unemployed, lower status individuals were substantially more likely to be stopped repeatedly. Many of the same groups — plus Afro-Caribbeans — were more likely to be searched and less likely to think they were treated politely. The most common complaints about policing concerned rude, arrogant, and racist behaviour, along with unjustified stops and the undue use of force, and these were even more common among Afro-Caribbeans. From the point of view of the public, all of these experiences could reinforce their sense of being subject to undue surveillance, especially in light of the low rate at which arrests actually were made and the weak relationship between stops, searches, and arrests. These street enforcement patterns seem to have widened the gulf between ethnic minorities and the police.

4 Responsibilities of the public

Crime is not solely the responsibility of the police; the problem is too large and complex for them to handle on their own. The police are largely reactive; they need to be 'mobilised' so that they can respond to problems. It is their responsibility to come quickly if the situation warrants it, deal with immediate crises, interview potential witnesses, and search diligently for clues. This report has also documented some of the benefits of their keeping victims informed, and treating potential suspects in civil fashion.

On their part, the public has to stand ready to provide the police with timely and complete information. They need to report crimes when they happen, convey their suspicions when they think something is about to happen, and be ready to provide information and stand as witnesses when police conduct their investigations. The 1988 BCS indicates that, whilst many are doing their part, a significant percentage of the population could do more.

Reporting crime

One of the most basic responsibilities of the public is to inform the police when crime occurs. However, studies like the BCS indicate that large amounts of often serious crime are not brought to the attention of the authorities. Participants in the 1988 survey were questioned extensively about their crime experiences.[1] The survey revealed that only about 37 per cent of victims had contacted the police about the matter. Most of them summoned the police themselves or had someone else do it for them, using 999 or by telephoning a police station directly. The police typically were summoned when losses were extensive (the highest level of reporting was for car theft), and for burglary. Reporting was low for personal crimes, especially assault. The reporting rates for different categories of incident are presented in Table 12.

Victims interviewed in the BCS gave a number of reasons for non-reporting. It appears, for example, that victims undertake a kind of personal cost-benefit analysis of their predicament. They do not report their experiences to police when their losses are nil or seem too trivial to warrant reporting; this reason was given by 48 per cent of those who indicated why they did not make an official crime report. Victims also do not report when they believe they will not get their property back or when they judge the offender is unlikely to be caught; 21 per cent indicated they did not report because 'the police could do nothing'. In

---

[1]This analysis is based on incidents recalled by all BCS respondents. For a detailed discussion of reporting to police, see Mayhew, Elliott, and Dowds, 1989.

addition, victims who are not particularly upset about what happened to them often do not make an effort to contact the police. Fear of reprisal was rarely mentioned (one per cent) by victims. Negative feelings toward the *police* also played a very limited role in these decisions. Observations that the police would not want to be bothered by them or would not have been interested in their case made up only about ten per cent of the reasons victims gave for non-reporting, and only one per cent pointed to a dislike or fear of the police. In the 1984 BCS, victims' feelings toward police were relevant only for the reporting of less serious incidents (Hough and Mayhew, 1985; see also Skogan, 1984, for a summary of research).

Table 12

Percentage of incidents for which police were contacted

Offence type	per cent reported	(N)
vehicle theft	95	(281)
completed house burglary	86	(377)
attempted/no loss burglary	41	(555)
robbery, wounding and sexual assault	42	(171)
theft from vehicles	40	(1284)
all personal crime	34	(1015)
threats to kill/assault/intimidate	37	(289)
common assault	33	(302)
vehicle vandalism	22	(441)
house vandalism	26	(274)
theft in and around home	26	(797)
ALL INCIDENTS		
including thefts	37	(5304)
excluding thefts	37	(5015)

Weighted data; incident base

Crime reporting varies little between different social groups. There was a tendency in the BCS for women and older victims to report assaults, threats, and other personal crimes more often, and for higher-income victims to report simple property thefts more frequently. Asian and Afro-Caribbean victims were somewhat *more* likely than others to report property losses, in part because they tended to suffer larger losses (Mayhew, Elliott, and Dowds, 1989). Other studies typically find no differences in reporting by race, and not much ethnic difference in the reasons given for non-reporting (Skogan, 1984; Tuck and Southgate, 1981). Race was unrelated to patterns of reporting in personal crime.

As a result of non-reporting, there is a great deal of crime which does not come

45

to the notice of the police, and not all of it is trivial. Out of all crimes covered in the BCS, some 63 per cent went unreported in 1988. A majority of crimes were reported only in the categories of vehicle theft (95 per cent), burglary (63 per cent), and bicycle theft (62 per cent).

Non-reporting has consequences. It conceals a considerable amount of criminal activity from the attention of the authorities, thus helping shield its perpetrators from arrest. In one study, almost half of those arrested for burglary were apprehended only because of the direct assistance of the public (Burrows, 1986a). Sometimes this assistance comes from bystanders or security officers, but most often it is provided by victims and their immediate relatives (cf. Burrows and Tarling, 1987). Not being able to identify and apprehend offenders in large numbers of cases may limit the deterrent capacity of the criminal justice system. It may also result — in places where reporting is particularly low — in the misallocation of police resources.

When the parties to an offence are linked to one another in continuing fashion, as in domestic assault, failing to report may sentence the victim to repeated abuse. Victim support schemes often identify their potential clientele through police reports and referrals, and victims of crimes which go unreported may be cut off from this form of assistance. In addition, public compensation of crime victims and private insurance reimbursement is usually precluded unless the police have been notified. Thus, there potentially are both individual and collective benefits to fuller reporting.

Any effort to increase reporting should take the reasons for victim non-reporting identified in the BCS to heart. To the extent reporting involves a cost-benefit calculation, efforts to reduce the cost through providing convenient mechanisms for dealing with the police (perhaps by taking some reports over the telephone when that is appropriate, or at a scheduled appointment) might bear fruit. Some police forces do this now. In terms of benefits there are many programmes toward which the police might steer victims, and some of the 'intangibles' of good police work.

The BCS indicates that there is a great deal to be done in this regard. Victims were asked if they had been kept informed by the police, and if officers told them about services for victims or informed them about their right to compensation. This kind of information sharing was *extremely* rare — for example, only six per cent recalled being told about compensation, and three per cent about other programmes for victims. These low figures undoubtedly reflect, at least in part, judgement by police about when it was *appropriate* to give out such information. However, those who were kept well informed or were told about victim programmes were much more satisfied with police service than the vast majority who were not. The police have a great deal else to give as well, including giving advice about insurance claims, moral support, and even protection. Of all victims who reported to the police, 21 per cent felt that the police were not interested in their case, which was the second largest source of dissatisfaction registered by victims ('they did not do enough' was the leading complaint, see above at Table 5). The third largest objection, voiced by 19 per cent of all victims, was that the police did not keep them informed about their case. This kind of inaction undermines many of the benefits of reporting, so it should be no surprise that many victims do not report.

Stepping forward as witnesses

Crime victims often fail to share information with the police about their own experiences. In addition, the BCS indicates that many members of the public are reluctant to act when they witness crimes against others. This inaction can have a particularly corrosive impact on the community. A fundamental assumption behind the Neighbourhood Watch movement is that members of the public *will* act as the eyes and ears of the police. Community-based crime prevention programmes assume that the public has a sufficient sense of territoriality and civic responsibility that they will at least summon the police, if not intervene in some other fashion, when they witnesses criminal incidents. Where this is lacking, Neighbourhood Watch cannot function[2]. Research also indicates that people are more likely to fear crime in public places if they feel that no one will come to their aid if they are threatened (Skogan, 1986). As a result, parks, shopping districts, car parks, and other public places can empty out quickly as the sun goes down. Finally, the role of bystanders is crucial in clearing up theft and burglary cases, which typically take place when property owners are not around, and in protecting the potential victims of street crime. Timely action by witnesses is called for in all these circumstances.

To examine the issue of bystander inaction, participants in the BCS were asked several questions about crimes they might have witnessed during the past five years. A number indicated that they had observed instances of shoplifting (11 per cent), vandalism (14 per cent), and 'serious fights' (19 per cent). A few had observed thefts from parked cars (three per cent). However, very few who had witnessed these incidents did anything in response. Instances of stealing from cars and vandalism were most frequently reported to the police (by 29 and 22 per cent of those who saw them, respectively), whilst shoplifting (at 12 per cent) and serious fights (eight per cent) were less often reported.

It is no surprise that these figures did not approach 100 per cent. Studies of both actual and deliberately stage crimes indicate that bystanders take action only about one quarter of the time. Those who do not act sometimes report that they were fearful of doing so, because they might be harmed in some way as a result. More often, they failed to report because it seemed inconvenient or difficult to do so. In many situations it also may be ambiguous whether or not an offence is taking place, and bystanders may be unsure whether the apparent victim would welcome their intervention (Mayhew, 1981); these factors could explain the low frequency with which fights are reported. Bystanders fear embarrassment and

---

[2]Participation in Neighbourhood Watch and some of its consequences are explored in Mayhew, Elliot, and Dowds, 1989.

social disapproval if they mistakenly intervene in what turns out to be a legitimate activity (Shapland and Vagg, 1987).

The small numbers who saw a more obvious theft or vandalism offence in progress, *and* who were willing to step forward, may place an upper limit on the deterrent effect of the criminal justice system. This is because, typically, the victim in such offences cannot indentify the offender. Successful indentification and prosecution requires a good witness.

Bystander non-reporting was not related to many social factors, other than a tendency for witnesses between 16 and 29 to report fewer instances of vandalism, theft, and serious fights. Otherwise, failing to step forward was not strongly related to gender, education, race, or class, and reporting did not differ much between urban and rural areas [3]. It even did not vary much by people's overall impressions of the quality of police service. Clearly, more research needs to be done on this issue. Compared to the volume of research on reporting by crime victims, we know relatively little about what motivates bystanders. The large number of potential witnesses uncovered by the BSC, if motivated to act, could greatly enhance the deterrent capacity of the criminal justice system.

---

[3]Smith (1983) and Tuck and Southgate (1981) found that youths and Afro-Caribbeans expressed less willingness to contact police to report crimes or (Smith, ibid) to serve as witnesses and give evidence, but this was on the basis of purely hypothetical questions.

5 Conclusions

Summary of findings

The 1988 sweep of the British Crime Survey points to a number of conclusions. The residents of England and Wales have extensive contact with the police. Over the course of a little more than a year, 56 per cent contacted the police themselves, and 15 per cent were involved in police initiated encounters. These contacts overlapped considerably, so in total about 59 per cent of those who were interviewed had an encounter of some sort with police. A comparison of the 1988 BCS with past surveys reveals no evidence that the Police and Criminal Evidence Act of 1984 had a substantial impact on the frequency of these contacts. It appears that only a few of them involved 'emergencies'. About two per cent of all police-public contacts during 1987 involved 999 calls concerning specific criminal incidents. All the contacts that people had with the police concerning crimes, disturbances, suspicious people, ringing alarms and the like, together accounted for less than one third of their encounters. Non-crime, non-emergency situations are the only form of contact that the majority of the public has with the police in a given year, although this percentage differs from place to place. In larger cities, a greater proportion of the contacts that people have with the police concern crime and suspicious or disturbing circumstances. This proportion reaches over 50 per cent of the total contact in inner city areas. How well they are served in these emergency and non-emergency situations is the basis of many people's judgments about their performance.

The public had a great deal of confidence in the police. When asked to rate their general performance, 85 per cent said it was 'good' or 'very good', and only four per cent rated it 'very poor'. Most people thought the police serving in their area were not much different from those in other parts of the country. 18 per cent thought they were better than elsewhere, whilst only five per cent thought they were worse. However, there is some reason to be concerned about the level of support for the police. Three sweeps of the BCS and independent opinion polls reveal there has been a steady erosion of confidence in the police. Since the first BCS in 1982, the percentage of the public giving them the highest marks has dropped from 43 per cent to only 25 per cent. Only a few have ever given the police extremely low ratings, but enthusiasm for their performance has been on the wane. This decline can be observed among most major social groupings, in almost all kinds of communities, and among crime victims.

Opinions about the police are shaped by people's own experiences, what they hear from others, and by what they see and read about them. The media had the most influence on those who had no direct contacts with the police, and also some effect upon those who did. Those who had contacted or were stopped by the police were more likely to rely on their own experience. Not all these experiences were positive; a fair number of those who came into contact with the police expressed dissatisfaction with the encounter. The most frequent source of discontent among those who had asked for assistance concerned the amount of effort (or the lack thereof) the police seemed to put into their case; next biggest source of dissatisfaction was with their ability to answer questions and solve problems. More than one in five of those who contacted the police by telephone reported they were 'dissatisfied' or 'very dissatisfied' with the way they handled the matter. A major finding of this report is that the nearer people's problems lay to the traditional core of the police function, the more dissatisfied they were. Those who contacted police about specific criminal incidents were the most unhappy with how their case was handled, followed by those who contacted police concerning disturbances and other public order problems. Twenty per cent of those who were stopped while in the car or were approached by police on the street felt they were treated 'impolitely' or 'very impolitely', and almost as many indicated that being stopped made them less favourable in their view toward the police. Over time, there also has been a large decline in confidence in the police in all of these groups – those who contact the police, the people caught up in street encounters, and crime victims.

The BCS suggests that there is a gap — probably mounting — between the public's expectations about the capacity of the police and their actual ability to deliver services. The survey pointed up the importance to some of making arrests and recovering property, but the long term trend in this regard is not encouraging. This and other research also suggests that the public has unrealistic expectations with regard to the dispatch of rapid response cars. They were more satisfied when police came to the scene, regardless of their reason for contacting them, but many forces are adopting graded response schemes which will reduce the frequency with which this happens in the future. The findings of this survey reiterate the importance of how police treat crime victims at the scene, and the importance of sharing information with them about their case and services which are available to them.

People's perceptions of how their problems were handled or how they were treated by the police were consistently related to such factors as age and gender, race and status, and whether they lived in towns or the country. These differences in perception were clearest in the most discretionary circumstances, those in which the police were relatively unfettered in deciding to act or not, and how to do so. There was some evidence that both police and public initiated contacts with the police had racially divisive consequences. Afro-Caribbeans were the most frequently and repeatedly stopped, they were more often searched, and they were the most dissatisfied with how politely they were treated. They were also less satisfied than whites with how their cases were handled when they contacted the police. Asians were not disproportionately stopped, but they were also more likely than whites to indicate that they were not treated politely, and they were also less satisfied with how their cases were handled when they contacted the police.

Finally, the public can do a great deal more to help the police deal with crime problems in their communities. The responsibility for responding to crime does not lie completely in the hands of the police; civilians have a great deal to contribute, and it seems as if they could do more. The police are principally a reactive force; they rely on the public to inform them of events and provide information about problems. However, the BCS found that witnesses of crimes *usually* fail to summon the police, and that even victims themselves frequently do not notify them about what had happened. The public are important 'eyes and ears' for the police, but the BCS indicates that too frequently they are not fulfilling this role. The report discusses some of the barriers to information sharing between the police and the public, and what the BCS reveals that may be useful in trying to lower them. Almost a decade ago, the Scarman report called for better relations between police and the public; however, surveys of public opinion suggest that since then the gulf between them has grown wider rather than narrower.

Appendix A

Methodological and statistical procedures

The BCS sample is large; the police supplement was administered to more than 6,000 persons, and some of the tables in this report are based on very large numbers. In addition, a large ethnic minority oversample was also drawn by interviewing residents of households in the vicinity of sample addresses when respondents indicated that an Asian or Afro-Caribbean lived there. Many of the phenomena of interest (such as pedestrian encounters) also were quite infrequent. However, the BCS was clustered; parliamentary constituencies were sampled, then wards and polling districts were selected, addresses were sampled at the polling district level, and individual respondents were chosen for questioning at those addresses. In addition, residents of inner city areas were deliberately oversampled to improve the efficiency of estimates of victimization rates.

The impact of these sampling procedures on the *percentages* presented in this report was minimised by weighting each respondent to correct the data for the various deliberate over-representations. Except for tabulations by race, all of the tables in this report are based on the main sample and describe the adult population of England and Wales. This includes the percentages labelled 'all respondents'. However, the *margin of likely error* surrounding these percentages was not corrected by the weights, and, in fact, was inflated by both the sampling and weighting procedures. The 'design effect' on the magnitude of the errors was approximately 1.25 for the kind of issues being examined here. Ordinarily, social researchers insist that the difference between two (estimated) percentages be large enough that only in five samples out of 100 should such a difference appear due to the vagaries of sampling; this is the '$p < .05$' standard. The effect of a design factor of 1.25 is such that it can be accommodated by tightening that standard to '$p < .04$'. This was the level of statistical significance employed in the bivariate and multivariate analyses presented in this report. The tables flag individual relationships for their bivariate significance and for their significance controlling for other variables in the table. In every case the more conservative two-tailed test was utilised. The multivariate analyses utilised unweighted data, and because they were always concerned with the effects of race they always included the ethnic minority booster sample. The statistical significance of ethnicity was tested separately for Afro-Caribbeans and Asians; in each case, they were benchmarked against the majority white population.

Statistical significance should not be confused with substantive significance or policy relevance. Tuck and Southgate (1981) examined the frequency of stops, searches, and arrests in Manchester, by ethnicity. They found a ratio of Afro-Caribbean to white stops of 1.4:1, but this difference was not significant given the size of their sample (slightly over 800) and they correctly disregarded it. In the 1988 BCS, the ratio of Afro-Caribbean to white street stops was 1.3;1, but this finding was based on over 5,000 respondents and was very significant. Is this difference — smaller than Tuck and Southgate's — of interest? That is not a statistical question, but one that the reader must answer.

Multivariate analysis

Several tables in Appendix B present the results of multivariate statistical analyses. The co-efficients are estimates of the differences in the *probability* of being in the category of the dependent variable that is of interest (for example, being stopped by police) that is attributable to being in a particular category of an independent variable, separate from the effects of the other explanatory variables. Expressing the effects of the independent variables in this way makes them easily interpretable: each respondent's chance of being in a category of the dependent variable ranges from 0 to 1, and is moved fractionally up or down due to the (estimated) effects of his or her standing on the explanatory variables. For example, the size of place of residence was represented by five categories, ranging from 'inner city' to 'rural area', so the co-efficients associated with their variable estimate the effect of moving up or down one notch on the list. The effect of ethnicity was estimated by including dummy variables for Asians and Afro-Caribbeans, leaving whites (and 38 orientals) as the 'reference category' against which the role of minority status was assessed. These estimates were made using logistic regression in SYSTAT. Only significant co-efficients ($p < .04$) are presented in the tables, but the changes in probability still need to be read for their substantive significance.

The endogeneity problem

In non-experimental research it is always difficult to interpret what it means to 'control' for a factor. For example, Table B-8 examines the joint impact of demographic factors (age; ethnicity; gender) and lifestyle factors (driving habits; evenings out; past arrests) on the risk of being stopped by police. When the latter are introduced, the apparent effects of some of the former are reduced. However, lifestyle factors like 'going out at night' and 'past arrests' are strongly dependent upon such demographic factors as gender and age. When some of the independent variables are in part caused by others, ordinary multivariate statistics *overestimate* the effect of the 'caused' (or 'endogeneous') independent variables and *underestimate* effects of the remaining ('exogeneous') independent variables. The indirect effects of the exogeneous factors, which pass via the endogeneous ones, get lost. Thus, Table B-8 suggests that the effect of being Asian 'disappears' when (endogeneous) lifestyle factors are taken into account, although in fact it has not. One solution to this problem is to analyze the data using two-stage least squares regression; another is to specify each problem as a causal model and estimate both the direct and indirect effects of the exogeneous explanatory variables. A more descriptive approach was adopted here. Tables which have clear endogeneity problems present two sets of findings: one represents the effects of the demographic variables, and the second adds obviously endogeneous explanatory variables. Differences between the two can be loosely interpreted as representing the effects of the intermediating factors. Of course, what is endogeneous is itself a complex question, and some will argue that factors like ethnicity are causes of other 'demographic' features like educational attainment and nature of the area in which people live. However, for the purpose of examining the distribution of recent and episodic events like contact with the police, such deep considerations of cause are unnecessary. It is just the fleeting effects of current activity patterns, recreational pursuits, and the like that we wish to avoid confusing with those of more fundamental social divisions.

Appendix B

Selected detailed tabulations

Table B-1
Changes in attitudes toward police

	Per cent 'very good job'			(N)		
	1982	1984	1988	1982	1984	1988
ETHNICITY						
whites	44	34	26	8705	9702	4067
Afro-Caribbean	27	26	16	63	141	365
Asian	36	35	16	133	118	605
AGE						
16-24	25	20	15	1386	1549	640
25-29	31	20	15	830	818	359
30-44	40	30	21	2501	2716	1160
45-59	46	37	28	1990	2369	1017
60 plus	58	46	37	2373	2641	1052
GENDER						
males	41	32	24	4305	5021	2090
females	45	35	27	4805	5130	2158
AREA						
inner/metro	37	27	21	3124	3812	1512
urbanised	41	34	25	1598	1967	813
mixed/rural	48	39	29	4389	4390	1823

Weighted data from three sweeps of the BCS. The area categories are not strictly comparable from survey to survey.

Table B-2
Detailed correlates of public initiated contacts

Percentage of each group who:-

	Telephoned 999	Visited Station	Approached in public	Other	(N)
ETHNICITY					
whites	9	26	24	23	15	(4656)
Afro-Caribbean	13*	16*	28	27	12	(513)
Asian	14*	17*	23	14*	8*	(747)
AGE	*	*	*		*	*
16-24	6	21	33	25	17	(722)
25-29	10	31	30	26	14	(408)
30-44	10	36	28	28	19	(1290)
45-59	12	31	24	24	17	(1148)
60 plus	7	14	11	15	8	(1266)
INCOME		*	*	*	*	
under £10,000	9	19	19	19	11	(1805)
£10-20,000	10	35	28	28	19	(1179)
over £20,000	11	42	34	34	25	(615)
OCCUPATION		*	*	*	*	
semi-unskilled	9	17	20	17	10	(986)
skilled	8	22	22	22	13	(1381)
non-managerial	10	31	24	26	17	(854)
professional	10	35	28	28	20	(1388)
HOUSING		*	*	*	*	
council	10	18	19	19	11	(1061)
all others	9	28	25	24	16	(3797)
AREA TYPE	*			*	*	
inner city	14	24	23	22	12	(846)
metropolitan	10	25	23	19	13	(1041)
urbanised	10	25	24	23	16	(972)
mixed areas	6	28	26	24	18	(1091)
rural areas	8	28	22	27	15	(958)
AGE LEFT SCHOOL		*	*	*	*	
under age 15	8	13	12	14	9	(1167)
all others	9	30	28	26	17	(3642)
GENDER		*	*	*		
males	9	28	31	29	17	(2340)
females	10	24	17	18	14	(2518)

Table B-2 (continued)

Detailed correlates of public initiated contacts

Percentage of each group who:-

	Telephoned 999	Visited Station	Station	Approached in public	Other	(N)
VICTIMISATION	*	*	*	*		
non-victim	7	19	17	20	4	(3024)
victim	14	38	34	28	6	(1829)
TOTAL	9	26	24	23	15	(4858)
(N)	(450)	(1269)	(1156)	(1125)	(234)	

Weighted data. The value of N varies slightly from column to column. *indicates a significant bivariate relationship.

Table B-3

Analysis of public initiated contacts: Changes in probability associated with the independent variables

GROUP	Public initiated contact		Multiple public contacts	
	(a)	(b)	(a)	(b)
Afro-Caribbean				
Asian	−.16	−.15	−.08	−.08
age	−.04	−.03		
high job status	+.04	−.03	+.02	+.02
council housing	−.04			
male	+.14	+.14	+.03	
size of area			−.01	−.02
education	+.03	+.03		
victim	—	+.23	—	+.04
(N)	(5706)	(5610)	(3315)	(3256)

Unweighted data. Probabilities which are not significant p < .04 are excluded. The 'a' columns exclude the victimisation measure; the 'b' columns include the victimisation measure in the analysis. Group definitions can be found in Tables B-2 and B-7.

Table B-4
Percentage of specific complaints by types of contact

| Nature of complaint | Type of contact | | | |
| | Telephoned | | Visited | Spoke to |
	999	Station	station	in public
1. APPARENT LACK OF EFFORT	59	62	50	36
(i) were not interested	27	36	32	19
(ii) did not do enough	41	42	28	25
2. POOR PERFORMANCE	16	15	28	27
(i) could not answer query	2	3	7	15
(ii) made mistakes	6	4	13	8
(iii) did not apprehend anyone	11	7	6	6
(vi) did not recover property	–	4	5	2
3. MADE RESPONDENT WAIT	24	14	10	2
4. DID NOT KEEP INFORMED	11	12	9	10
5. BEHAVED IMPOLITELY	5	3	12	25
6. OTHER	17	23	28	28
(N)	(63)	(182)	(184)	(44)

Weighted data. Percentages sum to more than 100 per cent by column because respondents could register more than one type of dissatisfaction.

Table B-5
Satisfaction with public Initiated contacts (for 999 and police station telephone contacts only)

Changes in probability associated with the independent variables

	Dissatisfaction	Met when telephoned	Telephoned about Crime	Telephoned about Disturbances
Afro-Caribbean	+.11			−.13
Asian	+.11			−.08
unemployed	+.07		+.08	
male	+.06	+.08		−.04
age	−.06		−.01	+.08
education	−.02			
size of area			−.03	−.02
high job status				
council housing				
about crime	+.19	+.06	—	—
about disturbance	+.17	−.07	—	—
about information	+.06	−.14	—	—
met police when telephoned	−.09	—	—	—
(N)	(1125)	(1147)	(1199)	(1199)

Unweighted data. Probabilities which are not significant p < .04 are excluded. The 'dissatisfaction' measure is coded high if fairly or very dissatisfied with either a 999 or police station telephone contact. Group definitions can be found in Tables B-2 and B-7.

Table B-6
Information sources and attitudes towards police

Changes in probability associated with the independent variables controlling for nine demographic and local variables

Information source	General assessments Rate police service as:		Public-initiated contacts was satisfied or very satisfied
	good/very good	above average	
own/others' experience	− .08	− .03	− .08
television and radio	+ .04	+ .02	+ .04
local/national newspapers	+ .05	+ .01	+ .03
(N)	(4144)	(3537)	(2693)

Unweighted data. All of these probabilities are significant p < .04. This table controls for race, age, gender, employment, education, area of residence, marital status, occupational status, and area housing conditions. 'Casual conversations' as a source of information were never significant, and are excluded here.

Table B-7
Detailed correlates of police initiated contacts

Percentage of each demographic group experiencing the following types of contact:			
traffic	*pedestrian*	*other*	*(N)*
ETHNICITY			
whites	11	3	3	(4655)
Afro-Caribbean	16*	5*	2	(513)
Asian	12	2	1	(748)
AGE	*	*		
16-24	26	10	3	(725)
25-29	16	3	2	(410)
30-44	13	1	2	(1294)
45–59	9	2	2	(1149)
60 plus	2	1	1	(1274)
INCOME	*			
under £10,000	7	1	2	(1802)
£10-20,000	12	2	2	(1179)
over £20,000	18	2	2	(616)
OCCUPATION	*			
semi/unskilled	10	3	3	(990)
skilled	10	2	2	(1386)
non-managerial	12	3	2	(858)
professional	15	3	2	(1394)
EMPLOYMENT	*	*		
unemployed	15	7	3	(577)
all others	11	2	2	(4301)
HOUSING	*			
council	9	4	1	(1067)
all others	12	3	2	(3804)
AGE LEFT SCHOOL	*	*		
under age 15	3	1	2	(1775)
all others	14	3	2	(3653)
GENDER	*	*		
males	16	4	3	(2528)
females	8	1	2	(2350)
MARITAL STATUS	*	*		
all others	9	1	2	(3854)
never married	21	8	3	(1013)

Table B-7
Detailed correlates of police initiated contacts (continued)

Percentage of each demographic group experiencing the following types of contact:

	traffic	pedestrian	other	(N)
AREA TYPE				
inner city	11	4	2	(851)
metropolitan	11	2	2	(1045)
urbanised	12	3	2	(928)
mixed areas	13	3	3	(1092)
rural areas	11	2	2	(961)
AREA HOUSING		*		
rated good	11	2	2	(3231)
rated fair	12	3	2	(1360)
bad/very bad	15	6	4	(153)
VEHICLE ACCESS	*			
has vehicle	14	3	2	(3760)
no vehicle	3	3	2	(1118)
PAST ARRESTS	*	*		
arrest in 5 yrs	23	8	3	(262)
not arrested	11	2	2	(4588)
TOTAL	12	3	2	(4856)
(N)	(563)	(137)	(102)	

Weighted data. The value of N varies slightly from column to column. * indicates a significant bivariate relationship.

TableB-8
Analysis of police initiated contacts

Changes in probability associated with the independent variables

Group	Police initiated contact (a)	(b)	Multiple police contacts (a)	(b)
Afro-Caribbean	+ .02	+ .03		
Asian	− .04		− .07	
age 16-24	+ .10	+ .10		
high job status	+ .02		+ .04	+ .04
council housing				
male	+ .09	+ .04	+ .12	+ .10
size of area				
education	+ .01			
never married	+ .06	+ .05	+ .07	+ .06
unemployed	+ .03	+ .03		
access to vehicle	+ .11	+ .04	+ .10	
evenings out	—	+ .02	—	+ .02
miles driven	—	+ .05	—	+ .03
past arrest	—	+ .07	—	
(N)	(5738)	(5680)	(815)	(808)

Unweighted data. Probabilities which are not significant p < .04 are excluded. The 'a' columns exclude the lifestyle measures; the 'b' columns include the liftestyle measures in the analysis. Group definitions can be found in Tables B-2 and B-7.

Table B-9
Correlates of discretionary actions by police

Changes in probability associated with the independent variables

| | Traffic stops | | Pedestrian encounters | |
	searched	treated politely	searched	treated politely
BY GROUP:				
Afro-Caribbeans	+ .14	− .06		− .15
Asians				
males	− .07		+ .20	
youths	+ .08	− .05		− .31
unemployed			+ .15	
housing bad	+ .05		+ .09	
size of area		− .10		
past arrest	+ .06		+ .12	
BY POLICE ACTION:				
searched	—	− .16	—	− .26
sanctioned	—	− .09	—	− .07
reason given	—	+ .11	—	+ .41
(N)	(709)	(661)	(169)	(162)

Unweighted combined sample. Probabilities which are not significant p < .04 are excluded. 'Police polite' coded high if they were rated polite or very polite. Group definitions can be found in Tables B-2 and B-7.

References

Box, S., Hale, S. and Andrews, G. (1988). 'Explaining fear of crime'. *British Journal of Criminology*, 28 pp. 340-355.

British Public Opinion. London: Market & Opinion Research International (May).

Brown, D. (1988). 'The police complaints procedure: a 'consumer' view'. *The Howard Journal*, 27, pp. 161-171.

Brown, D. (1988). *Detention at the Police Station under the Police and Criminal Evidence Act 1984.* Home Office Research Study No. 104. London HMSO.

Burrows, J. (1986a). *Burglary: police actions and victims' views.* Research and Planning Unit Paper No. 37. London Home Office.

Burrows, J. (1986b). 'Burglary investigations: victims' views of police activity'. *Policing*, 2, pp. 172-183.

Burrows, J. and Tarling, R. (1987). 'The investigation of crime in England and Wales'. *British Journal of Criminology*, 27, pp. 229-251.

Clarke, R. and Hough, M. (1984). *Crime and Police Effectiveness.* Home Office Research Study No. 79. London HMSO.

Ekblom, P. and Heal, K. (1982). *The Police Response to Calls from the Public.* Research and Planning Unit Paper No. 9. London: Home Office.

Gottfredson, M. (1984). *Victims of Crime: the dimensions of risk.* Home Office Research Study No. 78. London: HMSO.

Home Office. (1990) *Statistical Bulletin: statistics on the operation of certain police powers under the Police and Criminal Evidence Act, England and Wales,* (1989). London: HMSO.

Hough, M. (1987). 'Thinking about effectiveness'. *British Journal of Criminology*, 27, pp. 70-79.

Hough, M. (1989). 'Demand for policing and police performance: progress and pitfalls in public surveys'. In Weatheritt, M. (Ed.), *Police Research: some future prospects.* Farnborough: Avebury.

Hough, M. and Mayhew, P. (1983). *The British Crime Survey: first report.* Home Office Research Study No. 76. London: HMSO.

Hough, M. and Mayhew, P. (1985). *Taking Account of Crime: key findings from the 1984 British Crime Survey.* Home Office Research Study No. 85. London: HMSO.

Jones, S. (1983). 'Community Policing in Devon and Cornwall: some research findings on the relationship between the public and police'. In Bennett, T. (Ed.), *The Future of Policing.* Cambridge: Cropwood Conference Series No. 15.

Jones, T., Maclean, B. and Young, J. (1986). *The Islington Crime Survey.* Aldershot: Gower.

Kinsey, R. (1985). *Final Report of the Merseyside Crime Survey.* Liverpool: Merseyside County Council.

Maguire, M. (1984). *Burglary in a Dwelling.* London: Heinemann.

Maguire, M. (1988). 'Effects of the 'P.A.C.E.' provisions on detention and questioning'. *British Journal of Criminology* 28, pp. 19-43.

Manning, P. (1986). 'British Policing: continuities and change'. *The Howard Journal,* 25, pp. 261-278.

Mayhew, P. (1981). 'Crime in public view: surveillance and crime prevention'. In Brantingham, P. and Brantingham, P. (Eds.), *Environmental Criminology.* Newbury Park, CA: Sage Publications.

Maxfield, M. (1988). 'The London Metropolitan Police and their clients: victim and suspect attitudes'. *Journal of Research in Crime and Delinquency* 25, pp. 188-206.

Moxon, D. and Jones, P. (1984). 'Public reactions to police behaviour: some findings from the British Crime Survey'. *Policing* 1 pp. 49-56.

Newburn, T. (1989). 'The police, victims and victim support'. *Research and Planning Unit Research Bulletin* 26, pp. 22-25. London: Home Office.

Reiner, R. (1985). *The politics of the Police.* New York: St Martin's Press.

Shapland, J. (1984). 'Victims, the criminal justice system and compensation'. *British Journal of Criminology,* 24, pp. 131-149.

Skogan, W. (1984). 'Reporting crimes to police: the status of world research'. *Journal of Research in Crime and Delinquency,* 21, pp. 113-137.

Skogan, W. (1986). 'Fear of crime and neighbourhood change'. In Reiss, A. and Tonry, M. (Eds.), *Communities and Crime.* Chicago: University of Chicago Press.

Skokgan, W. and Antunes, G. (1979). 'Information, apprehension and deterrence: exploring the limits of police productivity'. *Journal of Criminal Justice,* 1979, pp. 217-242.

Smith, D. J. (1983). *Police and people in London I: a survey of Londoners.* London: Policy Studies Institute.

Southgate, P. and Ekblom, P. (1984). *Contacts between Police and Public: findings from the British Crime Survey.* Home Office Research Study No. 77. London: HMSO.

Sparks, R., Genn, H. and Dodd, D.J. (1977). *Surveying Victims.* London: John Wiley.

Tuck, M. and Southgate, P. (1981). *Ethnic Minorities, Crime and Policing: a survey of the experiences of West Indians and whites.* Home Office Research Study No. 70. London: HMSO.

Tyler, T. and Lind, E.A. (1988). *The Social Psychology of Procedural Justice.* New York: Plenum.

Willis, C. (1983). *The Use, Effectiveness and Impact of Police Stop and Search Powers.* Research and Planning Unit Paper No. 15. London: Home Office.

Publications

Titles already published for the Home Office

Studies in the Causes of Delinquency and the Treatment of Offenders (SCDTO)

1. Prediction methods in relation to borstal training. Hermann Mannheim and Leslie T. Wilkins. 1955. viii + 276pp. (11 340051 9).
2. *Time spent awaiting trial. Evelyn Gibson. 1960. v + 45pp. (34-368-2).
3. *Delinquent generations. Leslie T. Wilkins. 1960. iv + 20pp. (11 340053 5).
4. *Murder. Evelyn Gibson and S. Klein. 1961. iv + 44pp. (11 340054 3).
5. Persistent criminals. A study of all offenders liable to preventive detention in 1956. W. H. Hammond and Edna Chayen. 1963. ix + 237pp. (34-368-5).
6. *Some statistical and other numerical techniques for classifying individuals. P. McNaughton-Smith. 1965. v + 33pp. (34-368-6).
7. Probation research: a preliminary report. Part I. General outline of research. Part II. Study of Middlesex probation area (SOMPA). Steven Folkard, Kate Lyon, Margaret M. Carver and Erica O'Leary. 1966. vi + 58pp. (11 340374 7).
8. *Probation research: national study of probation. Trends and regional comparisions in probation (England and Wales). Hugh Barr and Erica O'Leary. 1966. vii + 51pp. (34-368-8).
9. *Probation research: a survey of group work in the probation service. Hugh Barr. 1966. vii + 94pp. (34-368-9).
10. *Types of delinquency and home background. A validation study of Hewitt and Jenkins' hypothesis. Elizabeth Field. 1967. vi + 21pp. (34-368-10).
11. *Studies of female offenders. No. 1–Girls of 16-20 years sentenced to borstal or detention centre training in 1963. No. 2–Women offenders in the Metropolitan Police District in March and April 1957. No. 3–A description of women in prison on January 1, 1965. Nancy Goodman and Jean Price. 1967. v + 78pp. (34-368-11).
12. *The use of the Jesness Inventory on a sample of British probationers. Martin Davies. 1967. iv + 20pp. (34-368-12).
13. *The Jesness Inventory: application to approved school boys. Joy Mott. 1969. iv + 27pp. (11 340063 2).

Home Office Research Studies (HORS)

1. *Workloads in children's departments. Eleanor Grey. 1969. vi + 75pp. (11 340101 9).
2. *Probationers in their social environment. A study of male probationers aged 17-20, together with an analysis of those reconvicted within twelve months. Martin Davies. 1969. vii + 204pp. (11 340102 7).
3. *Murder 1957 to 1968. A Home Office Statistical Division report on murder in England and Wales. Evelyn Gibson and S. Klein (with annex by the Scottish Home and Health Department on murder in Scotland). 1969. vi + 94pp. (11 340103 5).
4. Firearms in crime. A Home Office Statistical Division report on indictable offences involving firearms in England and Wales. A. D. Weatherhead and B. M. Robinson. 1970. viii + 39pp. (11 340104 3).
5. *Financial penalties and probation. Martin Davies. 1970. vii + 39pp. (11 340105 1).
6. *Hostels for probationers. A study of the aims, working and variations in effectiveness of male probation hostels with special reference to the influence of the environment on delinquency. Ian Sinclair. 1971. ix + 200pp. (11 340106 X).

---

*Out of Print

7. *Prediction methods in criminology–including a prediction study of young men on probation. Frances H. Simon. 1971. xi + 234pp.   (11 340107 8).

8. *Study of the juvenile liaison scheme in West Ham 1961-65. Marilyn Taylor. 1971. vi + 46pp.   (11 340108 6).

9. *Explorations in after-care. I–After-care units in London, Liverpool and Manchester. Martin Silberman (Royal London Prisoners' Aid Society) and Brenda Chapman. II–After-care hostels receiving a Home Office grant. Ian Sinclair and David Snow (HORU). III–St. Martin of Tours House. Aryeh Leissner (National Bureau for Co-operation in Child Care). 1971. xi + 140pp.   (11 340109 4).

10. A survey of adoption in Great Britain. Eleanor Grey in collaboration with Ronald M. Blunden. 1971. ix + 168pp.   (11 340110 8).

11. *Thirteen-year-old approved school boys in 1962. Elizabeth Field, W. H. Hammond and J. Tizard. 1971. ix + 46pp.   (11 340111 6).

12. Absconding from approved schools. R. V. G. Clarke and D. N. Martin. 1971. vi + 146pp.   (11 340112 4).

13. An experiment in personality assessment of young men remanded in custody. H. Sylvia Anthony. 1972. viii + 79pp.   (11 340113 2).

14. *Girl offenders aged 17-20 years. I - Statistics relating to girl offenders aged 17-20 years from 1960 to 1970. II - Re-offending by girls released from Borstal or detention centre training. III - The problems of girls released from borstal training during their period on after-care. Jean Davies and Nancy Goodman. 1972. v + 77pp.   (11 340114 0).

15. *The controlled trial in institutional research - paradigm or pitfall for penal evaluators? R. V. G. Clarke and D. B. Cornish. 1972. v + 33pp.   (11 340115 9).

16. *A survey of fine enforcement. Paul Softley. 1973. v + 65pp.   (11 340116 7).

17. *An index of social environment - designed for use in social work research. Martin Davies. 1973. vi + 63pp.   (11 340117 5).

18. *Social enquiry reports and the probation service. Martin Davies and Andrea Knopf. 1973. v + 49pp.   (11 340118 3).

19. *Depression, psychopathic personality and attempted suicide in a Borstal sample. H. Sylvia Anthony. 1973. viii + 44pp.   (0 11 340119 1).

20. *The use of bail and custody by London magistrates' courts before and after the Criminal Justice Act 1967. Frances Simon and Mollie Weatheritt. 1974. vi + 78pp.   (0 11 340120 5).

21. *Social work in the environment. A study of one aspect of probation practice. Martin Davies, with Margaret Rayfield, Alaster Calder and Tony Fowles. 1974. ix + 151pp.   (0 11 340121 3).

22. Social work in prison. An experiment in the use of extended contact with offenders. Margaret Shaw. 1974. viii + 154pp.   (0 11 340122 1).

23. Delinquency amongst opiate users. Joy Mott and Marilyn Taylor. 1974. vi + 31pp. (0 11 340663 0).

24. IMPACT. Intensive matched probation and after-care treatment. Vol. I - The design of the probation experiment and an interim evaluation. M. S. Folkard, A. J. Fowles, B. C. McWilliams, W. McWilliams, D. D. Smith, D. E. Smith and G. R. Walmsley. 1974. v + 54pp. (0 11 340664 9).

25. The approved school experience. An account of boys' experiences of training under differing regimes of approved schools, with an attempt to evaluate the effectiveness of that training. Anne B. Dunlop. 1974. vii + 124pp.   (0 11 340665 7).

26. *Absconding from open prisons. Charlotte Banks, Patricia Mayhew and R. J. Sapsford. 1975. viii + 89pp.   (0 11 340666 5).

27. Driving while disqualified. Sue Kriefman. 1975. vi + 136pp. (0 11 340667 3).

28. Some male offenders' problems. I - Homeless offenders in Liverpool. W. McWilliams. II - Casework with short-term prisoners. Julie Holborn. 1975. x + 147pp.   (0 11 340668 1).

29. *Community service orders. K. Pease, P. Durkin, I. Earnshaw, D. Payne and J. Thorpe. 1975. viii + 80pp.   (0 11 340669 X).

30. Field Wing Bail Hostel: the first nine months. Frances Simon and Sheena Wilson. 1975. viii + 55pp. (0 11 340670 3).

31. Homicide in England and Wales 1967-1971. Evelyn Gibson. 1975. iv + 59pp. (0 11 340753 X).

*Out of Print

32. Residential treatment and its effects on delinquency. D. B. Cornish and R. V. G. Clarke. 1975. vi + 74pp. (0 11 340672 X).

33. Further studies of female offenders. Part A: Borstal girls eight years after release. Nancy Goodman, Elizabeth Maloney and Jean Davies. Part B: The sentencing of women at the London Higher Courts. Nancy Goodman, Paul Durkin and Janet Halton. Part C: Girls appearing before a juvenile court. Jean Davies. 1976. vi + 114pp. (0 11 340673 8).

34. *Crime as opportunity. P. Mayhew, R. V. G. Clarke, A. Sturman and J. M. Hough. 1976. vii + 36pp. (0 11 340674 6).

35. The effectiveness of sentencing: a review of the literature. S. R. Brody. 1976. v + 89pp. (0 11 340675 4).

36. IMPACT. Intensive matched probation and after-care treatment. Vol. II - The results of the experiment. M. S. Folkard, D. E. Smith and D. D. Smith. 1976. xi + 40pp. (0 11 340676 2).

37. Police cautioning in England and Wales. J. A. Ditchfield. 1976. v + 31pp. (0 11 340677 0).

38. Parole in England and Wales. C. P. Nuttall, with E. E. Barnard, A. J. Fowles, A. Frost, W. H. Hammond, P. Mayhew, K. Pease, R. Tarling and M. J. Weatheritt. 1977. vi + 90pp. (0 11 340678 9).

39. Community service assessed in 1976. K. Pease, S. Billingham and I. Earnshaw. 1977. vi + 29pp. (0 11 340679 7).

40. Screen violence and film censorship: a review of research. Stephen Brody. 1977. vii + 179pp. (0 11 340680 0).

41. *Absconding from borstals. Gloria K. Laycock. 1977. v + 82pp. (0 11 340681 9).

42. Gambling: a review of the literature and its implications for policy and research. D. B. Cornish. 1978. xii + 284pp. (0 11 340682 7).

43. Compensation orders in magistrates' courts. Paul Softley. 1978. v + 41pp. (0 11 340683 5).

44. Research in criminal justice. John Croft. 1978. iv + 16pp. (0 11 340684 3).

45. Prison welfare: an account of an experiment at Liverpool. A. J. Fowles. 1978. v + 34pp. (0 11 340685 1).

46. Fines in magistrates' courts. Paul Softley. 1978. v + 42pp. (0 11 340686 X).

47. Tackling vandalism. R. V. G. Clarke (editor), F. J. Gladstone, A. Sturman and Sheena Wilson (contributors). 1978. vi + 91pp. (0 11 340687 8).

48. Social inquiry reports: a survey. Jennifer Thorpe. 1979. vi + 55pp. (0 11 340688 6).

49. Crime in public view. P. Mayhew, R. V. G. Clarke, J. N. Burrows, J. M. Hough and S. W. C. Winchester. 1979. v + 36pp. (0 11 340689 4).

50. *Crime and the community. John Croft. 1979. v + 16pp. (0 11 340690 8).

51. Life-sentence prisoners. David Smith (editor), Christopher Brown, Joan Worth, Roger Sapsford and Charlotte Banks (contributors). 1979. iv + 51pp. (0 11 340691 6).

52. Hostels for offenders. Jane E. Andrews, with an appendix by Bill Sheppard. 1979. v + 30pp. (0 11 340692 4).

53. Previous convictions, sentence and reconviction: a statistical study of a sample of 5,000 offenders convicted in January 1971. G. J. O. Phillpotts and L. B. Lancucki. 1979. v + 55pp. (0 11 340693 2).

54. Sexual offences, consent and sentencing. Roy Walmsley and Karen White. 1979. vi + 77pp. (0 11 340694 0).

55. Crime prevention and the police. John Burrows, Paul Ekblom and Kevin Heal. 1979. v + 37pp. (0 11 340695 9).

56. Sentencing practice in magistrates' courts. Roger Tarling, with the assistance of Mollie Weatheritt. 1979. vii + 54pp. (0 11 340696 7).

57. Crime and comparative research. John Croft. 1979. iv + 16pp. (0 11 340697 5).

58. Race, crime and arrests. Philip Stevens and Carole F. Willis. 1979. v + 69pp. (0 11 340698 3).

59. Research and criminal policy. John Croft. 1980. iv + 14pp. (0 11 340699 1).

60. Junior attendance centres. Anne B. Dunlop. 1980. v + 47pp. (0 11 340700 9).

61. Police interrogation: an observational study in four police stations. Paul Softley, with the assistance of David Brown, Bob Forde, George Mair and David Moxon. 1980. vii + 67pp. (0 11 340701 7).

62. Co-ordinating crime prevention efforts. F. J. Gladstone. 1980. v + 74pp. (0 11 340702 5).

63. Crime prevention publicity: an assessment. D. Riley and P. Mayhew. 1980. v + 47pp. (0 11 340703 3).

*Out of Print

64. Taking offenders out of circulation. Stephen Brody and Roger Tarling. 1980. v + 46pp. (0 11 340704 1).
65. *Alcoholism and social policy: are we on the right lines? Mary Tuck. 1980. v + 30pp. (0 11 340705 X).
66. Persistent petty offenders. Suzan Fairhead. 1981. vi + 78pp.   (0 11 340706 8).
67. Crime control and the police. Pauline Morris and Kevin Heal. 1981. v + 71pp. (0 11 340707 6).
— 68. Ethnic minorities in Britain: a study of trends in their position since 1961. Simon Field, George Mair, Tom Rees and Philip Stevens. 1981. v + 48pp.   (0 11 340708 4).
69. Managing criminological research. John Croft. 1981. iv + 17pp.   (0 11 340709 2).
— 70. Ethnic minorities, crime and policing: a survey of the experiences of West Indians and whites. Mary Tuck and Peter Southgate. 1981. iv + 54pp.   (0 11 340765 3).
71. Contested trials in magistrates' courts. Julie Vennard. 1982. v + 32pp.   (0 11 340766 1).
72. Public disorder: a review of research and a study in one inner city area. Simon Field and Peter Southgate. 1982. v + 77pp.   (0 11 340767 X).
73. Clearing up crime. John Burrows and Roger Tarling. 1982. vii + 31pp.   (0 11 340768 8).
74. Residential burglary: the limits of prevention. Stuart Winchester and Hilary Jackson. 1982. v + 47pp.   (0 11 340769 6).
75. Concerning crime. John Croft. 1982. iv + 16pp.   (0 11 340770 X).
76. The British Crime Survey: first report. Mike Hough and Pat Mayhew. 1983. v + 62pp. (0 11 340786 6).
77. Contacts between police and public: findings from the British Crime Survey. Peter Southgate and Paul Ekblom. 1984. v + 42pp.   (0 11 340771 8).
78. Fear of crime in England and Wales. Michael Maxfield. 1984. v + 57pp.   (0 11 340772 6).
79. Crime and police effectiveness. Ronald V Clarke and Mike Hough. 1984. iv + 33pp. (0 11 340773 3).
— 80. The attitudes of ethnic minorities. Simon Field. 1984. v + 49pp.   (0 11 340774 2).
81. Victims of crime: the dimensions of risk. Michael Gottfredson. 1984. v + 54pp. (0 11 340775 0).
82. The tape recording of police interviews with suspects: an interim report. Carole Willis. 1984. v + 45pp.   (0 11 340776 9).
83. Parental supervision and juvenile delinquency. David Riley and Margaret Shaw. 1985. v + 90pp.   (0 11 340799 8).
84. Adult prisons and prisoners in England and Wales 1970-1982: a review of the findings of social research. Joy Mott. 1985. vi + 73pp.   (0 11 340801 3).
85. Taking account of crime: key findings from the 1984 British Crime Survey. Mike Hough and Pat Mayhew. 1985. vi + 115pp.   (0 11 341810 2).
86. Implementing crime prevention measures. Tim Hope. 1985. vi + 82pp.   (0 11 340812 9).
87. Resettling refugees. the lessons of research. Simon Field. 1985. vi + 66pp.   (0 11 340815 3).
88. Investigating burglary: the measurement of police performance. John Burrows. 1986. vi + 36pp.   (0 11 340824 2).
— 89. Personal violence. Roy Walmsley. 1986. vi + 87pp.   (0 11 340827 7).
90. Police-public encounters. Peter Southgate. 1986. vi + 150pp.   (0 11 340834 X).
91. Grievance procedures in prisons. John Ditchfield and Claire Austin. 1986. vi + 87pp. (0 11 340839 0).
92. The effectiveness of the Forensic Science Service. Malcolm Ramsay. 1987. v + 100pp. (0 11 340842 0).
93. The police complaints procedure: a survey of complainants' views. David Brown. 1987. v + 98pp.   (0 11 340853 6).
94. The validity of the reconviction prediction score. Denis Ward. 1987. vi + 46pp. (0 11 340882 X).
95. Economic aspects of the illicit drug market and drug enforcement policies in the United Kingdom. Adam Wagstaff and Alan Maynard. 1988. vii + 156pp.   (0 11 340883 8).
96. Schools, disruptive behaviour and delinquency: a review of literature. John Graham. 1988. v + 70pp.   (0 11 340887 0).
97. The tape recording of police interviews with suspects: a second interim report. Carole Willis, John Macleod and Peter Naish. 1988. vii + 97pp.   (0 11 340890 0).

*Out of Print

98. Triable-either-way cases: Crown Court or magistrates' court. David Riley and Julie Vennard. 1988. v + 52pp. (0 11 340891 9).
99. Directing patrol work: a study of uniformed policing. John Burrows and Helen Lewis. 1988. v + 66pp. (0 11 340891 9).
100. Probation day centres. George Mair. 1988. v + 44pp. (0 11 340894 3).
101. Amusement machines: dependency and delinquency. John Graham. 1988. v + 48pp. (0 11 340895 1).
102. The use and enforcement of compensation orders in magistrates' courts. Tim Newburn. 1988. v + 49pp. (0 11 340896 X).
103. Sentencing practice in the Crown Court. David Moxon. 1988. v + 90pp. (0 11 340902 8).
104. Detention at the police station under the Police and Criminal Evidence Act 1984. David Brown. 1988. v + 88pp. (0 11 340908 7).
105. Changes in rape offences and sentencing. Charles Lloyd and Roy Walmsley. 1989. vi + 53pp. (0 11 340910 9).
106. Concerns about rape. Lorna Smith. 1989. v + 48pp. (0 11 340911 7).
107. Domestic violence. Lorna Smith. 1989. v + 132pp. (0 11 340925 7).
108. Drinking and disorder: a study of non-metropolitan violence. Mary Tuck. 1989. v + 111pp. (0 11 340926 5).
109. Special security units. Roy Walmsley. 1989. v + 114pp. (0 11 340961 3).
110. Pre-trial delay: the implications of time limits. Patricia Morgan and Julie Vennard. 1989. v + 66pp. (0 11 340964 8).
111. The 1988 British Crime Survey. Pat Mayhew, David Elliott and Lizanne Dowds. 1989. v + 133pp. (0 11 340965 6)
112. The settlement of claims at the Criminal Injuries Compensation Board. Tim Newburn. 1989. v + 40pp. (0 11 340967 2)
— 113. Race, community groups and service delivery. Hilary Jackson and Simon Field. 1989. v + 62pp. (0 11 340972 9)
114. Money payment supervision orders: probation policy and practice. George Mair and Charles Lloyd. 1989. v + 40pp. (0 11 340971 0)
115. Suicide and self-injury in prison: a literature review. Charles Lloyd. 1990. v + 69pp. (0 11 3409745 5)
116. Keeping in Touch: police-victim communication in two areas. Tim Newburn and Susan Merry. 1990. v + 52pp. (0 11 340974 5)

ALSO

Designing out crime. R. V. G. Clarke and P. Mayhew (editors). 1980. viii + 186pp. (0 11 340732 7).
(This book collects, with an introduction, studies that were originally published in HORS 34, 47, 49, 55, 62 and 63 and which are illustrative of the 'situational' approach to crime prevention.)
Policing today. Kevin Heal, Roger Tarling and John Burrows (editors). 1985. v + 181pp. (0 11 340800 5).
(This book brings together twelve separate studies on police matters produced during the last few years by the Unit. The collection records some relatively little known contributions to the debate on policing.)
Managing Criminal Justice: a collection of papers. David Moxon (ed.). 1985. vi + 222pp. (0 11 340811 0).
(This book brings together a number of studies bearing on the management of the criminal justice system. It includes papers by social scientists and operational researchers working within the Research and Planning Unit, and academic researchers who have studied particular aspects of the criminal process.)
Situational Crime Prevention: from theory into practice. Kevin Heal and Gloria Laycock (editors). 1986. vii + 166pp. (0 11 340826 9).
(Following the publication of *Designing Out Crime*, further research has been completed on the theoretical background to crime prevention. In drawing this work together this book sets down some of the theoretical concerns and discusses the emerging practical issues. It includes contributions by Unit staff as well as academics from this country and abroad.)

*Out of Print

Communities and crime reduction. Tim Hope and Margaret Shaw (eds.). 1988. vii + 311pp. (11 340892 7).

(The central theme of this book is the possibility of preventing crime by building upon the resources of local communities and of active citizens. The specially commissioned chapters, by distinguished international authors, review contemporary research and policy on community crime prevention.)

New directions in police training. Peter Southgate (ed.). 1988. xi + 256pp. (11 340889 7).

(Training is central to the development of the police role, and particular thought and effort now go into making it more responsive to current needs—in order to produce police officers who are both effective and sensitive in their dealing with the public. This book illustrates some of the thinking and research behind these developments.)

The above HMSO publications can be purchased from Government Bookshops or through booksellers.

The following Home Office research publications are available on request from the Home Office Research and Planning Unit, 50 Queen Anne's Gate, London SW1H 9AT.

Research Unit Papers (RUP)

1. Uniformed police work and management technology. J. M. Hough. 1980.
2. Supplementary information on sexual offences and sentencing. Roy Walmsley and Karen White. 1980.
3. Board of visitor adjudications. David Smith, Claire Austin and John Ditchfield. 1981.
4. Day centres and probation. Suzan Fairhead, with the assistance of J. Wilkinson-Grey. 1981.

Research and Planning Unit Papers (RPUP)

5. Ethnic minorities and complaints against the police. Philip Stevens and Carole Willis. 1982.
6. *Crime and public housing. Mike Hough and Pat Mayhew (editors). 1982.
7. *Abstracts of race relations research. George Mair and Philip Stevens (editors). 1982.
8. Police probationer training in race relations. Peter Southgate. 1982.
9. *The police response to calls from the public. Paul Ekblom and Kevin Heal. 1982.
10. City centre crime: a situational approach to prevention. Malxolm Ramsay. 1982.
11. Burglary in schools: the prospects for prevention. Tim Hope. 1982.
12. *Fine enforcement. Paul Softley and David Moxon. 1982.
13. Vietnamese refugees. Peter Jones. 1982.
14. Community resources for victims of crime. Karen Williams. 1983.
15. The use, effectiveness and impact of police stop and search powers. Carole Willis. 1983.
16. Acquittal rates. Sid Butler. 1983.
17. Criminal justice comparisons: the case of Scotland and England and Wales. Lorna J. F. Smith. 1983.
18. Time taken to deal with juveniles under criminal proceedings. Catherine Frankenburg and Roger Tarling. 1983.
19. Civilian review of complaints against the police: a survey of the United States literature. David C. Brown. 1983.
20. Police action on motoring offences. David Riley. 1983.
21. *Diverting drunks from the criminal justice system. Sue Kingsley and George Mair. 1983.
22. The staff resource implications of an independent prosecution system. Peter R. Jones. 1983.
23. Reducing the prison population: an exploratory study in Hampshire. David Smith, Bill Sheppard, George Mair, Karen Williams. 1984.
24. Criminal justice system model: magistrates' courts sub-model. Susan Rice. 1984.
25. Measures of police effectiveness and efficiency. Ian Sinclair and Clive Miller. 1984.
26. Punishment practice by prison Boards of Visitors. Susan Iles, Adrienne Connors, Chris May, Joy Mott. 1984.
27. *Reparation, conciliation and mediation: current projects and plans in England and Wales. Tony Marshall. 1984.

*Out of Print

Research Bulletin

The Research Bulletin is published twice a year and consists mainly of short articles relating to projects which are part of the Home Office Research and Planning Unit's research programme.

---

*Out of Print

Printed in the UK by HMSO
821698   Dd. 0292894   C14   8/90   (P.P.)